THE OPEN BOOK SERIES

MEDIEVAL TIMES

Edited by Molly Lodge

Feudalism – Europe after Charlemagne – the Normans – Europe AD 1000 – Technology in the Middle Ages – International Trade – the Age of the Commune – Peasants in the Middle Ages – Science and Culture

HODDER AND STOUGHTON
LONDON SYDNEY AUCKLAND TORONTO

British Library Cataloguing in Publication Data

Lodge, Molly
    Medieval times. – (The open book series)
    1. Middle Ages – History – Juvenile literature
    I. Title
    909.07   D116

    ISBN 0-340-34193-9
    ISBN 0-340-33515-9 (Pbk)

Copyright © 1981 Gruppo Editoriale Fabbri S.p.A.,
Milano – Le Livre de Paris S.A. – Hachette,
Bagneux.

English language edition copyright © 1984
Hodder and Stoughton Ltd.

First published in this edition in Great Britain 1984.

Published by Hodder and Stoughton Children's Books,
a division of Hodder and Stoughton Ltd, Mill Road,
Dunton Green, Sevenoaks, Kent TN13 2YJ.

Photoset by Rowland Phototypesetting Ltd,
Bury St Edmunds, Suffolk.

Printed in Belgium by Henri Proost et Cie,
Turnhout.

'Everyone knows that I have nothing to eat and nothing to wear. Therefore, my Lord, I begged for your mercy, and in your generosity you have agreed to take me under your protection. I pledge my devotion and my services in return for these necessities of life . . .
As long as I live, and remain a free man, I will serve you faithfully. I shall not be able to resign from my duty to you, but in exchange I will pass the rest of my life under your power and protection.' This was the vassal's oath to his king.

Feudalism

THE COMPANION IN ARMS BECOMES THE 'KING'S MAN . . .'

In the great hall of the castle the king sits on his high wooden throne wearing ceremonial robes and a crown. Around him are knights and members of the court who will witness the ceremony. The presence of the bishop, holding a Bible, gives the proceedings a religious significance. The king and the companion in arms, or baron, will each swear on the Bible to keep his promise.

The baron, like all the king's companions in arms, is a powerful man. But his power and riches are nothing compared with those of the king. The king is in effect the sole rightful owner of the whole kingdom. He has inherited his lands or won them by conquest. He also holds political authority, invested in him in the name of the Church by a religious ceremony at the time of his coronation.

The baron recognises the supremacy of his king. He corroborates it when he swears the oath. Although he declares himself to be a free man, he promises to be a 'servant' of his king. He would have used the ancient Celtic word *gwass* or *wass*, which later became vassal, meaning 'servant'. When the vassal has sworn his oath he kneels before the king, who takes the baron's clasped hands in his own: it is an act of homage.

Then the king embraces the baron and tells him to rise. The allegiance of the new vassal is officially proclaimed. The brave companion in arms is now the 'king's man', and will remain in the king's service until he dies.

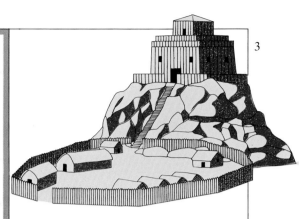

3

. . . and receives his protection

The king presents symbols of the privileges the vassal will receive in return for his allegiance. First, a clod of earth, representing the lands the vassal receives, and which he will administer in the name of his king. The lands are called a fief, from the Germanic word *fëhu*. The vassal who holds the lands by feudal tenure is a feudatory.

Then the branch of a green plant, to signify the productivity of the land. The branch has been cut off with an axe, to remind the vassal what will happen to his head if he betrays his king. Next the banner, with the king's colours mixed with those of the vassal, so that he will always remember who his real lord is. Finally a sword, symbol of the power of justice that the vassal will exercise in the name of his sovereign, and of his obligation to join him in battle.

THE EFFECTS OF FEUDALISM

The words of the vassal's oath at the beginning of this chapter are the earliest and most basic. In the years that followed, the oath became more complicated and the list of obligations, rights and reciprocal duties of the king and his vassal became more precise. Despite its simplicity, the original oath says all that needs to be said.

On the one hand there was the king, who needed trusted men on whom he could depend, who would help him with the administration of his land in times of peace and organise an army in times of war. On the other were the less powerful men, who wanted help and protection. The less powerful became faithful servants of the king, and he repaid them with a fief and certain privileges. For example, they were exempted from paying taxes, but were allowed to ask for taxes from their peasants; they could make laws, recruit soldiers, and wield power in other ways.

The feudal system organised society on a new basis. It was a network of relationships based on reciprocal help. It may seem surprising that this new system came into being so soon after the flowering of the great Carolingian Empire in Europe. But in effect the seed of feudalism was already sown under the Merovingian kings, including Charlemagne himself, who governed by entrusting parts of their territories to counts, marquises and dukes (from the Latin dux, *military chief).*

As we shall see, the successors of Charlemagne were not able to keep the Empire united, and this accelerated the change.

Internal conflicts, and savage attacks by warrior tribes (the Vikings from the north, the Hungarians from the east), threw Europe into total disorder.

The feudal system, which was born more from weakness and fear than from a precise plan of reform, was Europe's answer to these problems.

The most direct consequence of feudalism was the handing over to feudatories of responsibilities formerly held by the sovereign.

This transfer of land and power led to the kingdom being broken up into a large number of independent units, transferring the centre of social and economic activity from the town to the country: more precisely, to the baron's residence – the feudal castle around which lived the men and women over whom the feudal lord had absolute authority, apart from the priests.

The first feudal castles, based on the Roman castrum, *were built of wood and situated on a hill. The huts of the peasants under the protection of the baron nestled at the foot, surrounded by a palisade.*

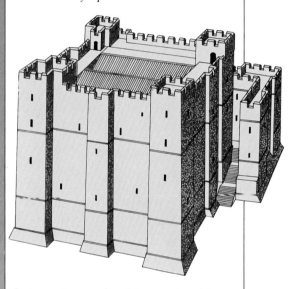

Later on stone replaced the wood, and the castle became a fortress with a defensive function.

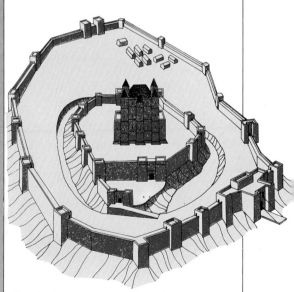

Finally the castle assumed its characteristic shape. More robust and complex, it enclosed all the people and activities connected with the feudal lord.

4 | *The castle was at the centre of a small enclosed community. It contained the living-quarters of the feudal lord, the soldiers, the peasants, the craftsmen and the serfs, as well as everything they needed: stables, store-rooms, shops, bakehouses, workshops . . . In an emergency it was possible to exist without contact with the outside world: the inhabitants could resist enemy assaults or attacks from more powerful feudal lords for a long time.*

The essential parts of a feudal castle were:
1. defensive ditch, or moat; 2. drawbridge;
3. portcullis; 4. turrets; 5. arrow slits;
6. room for working the drawbridge;
7. watch tower and soldiers' lodgings;
8. armoury; 9. courtyard with a well;
10. lodgings; 11. prison or dungeon;
12. store-rooms; 13. kitchens;
14. banqueting hall; 15. toilet;
16. suspended bridge; 17. cage for prisoners.

5

6

BARONS AND PAUPERS

Charlemagne died in 814, and the last emperor of the Carolingian dynasty, Charles the Fat, was deposed in 887.

In a little over seventy years the feudal system began to grow up in the ruins of the Carolingian Empire, in a disordered world constantly threatened by invasion.

It reached its peak during the twelfth century, in north-east and central Europe. The largest and most powerful fiefs eventually spread to become the principal modern states. Feudalism spread more slowly in Mediterranean Europe, particularly in Italy, where the city-states resisted the barons.

What was it like in a world where fear and need had engendered a system of personal relationships which today we would consider unjust, but which answered the needs of a society without telephones, roads, public services, and so on?

The feudal lord, 'king' of his fief

A fief was the territory conceded by the sovereign to his vassal. The vassal administered the land, but did not own it. He held the fief in usufruct; that is, he could use it for his own profit.

He benefited from the products of the land, from any taxes that he levied, and from any services of the inhabitants, but never became the real owner. On the death of the vassal the fief reverted, in principle, to the king.

However, normally the son or heir of the feudal lord succeeded him, renewing the oath of loyalty to the sovereign and thus taking over his father's fief.

This succession meant that the sovereign did not have much real power over the fief that he conceded to his vassal. If the vassal kept his oath and did not betray the trust the king had placed in him, he was the little king of his fief, and behaved like one.

The vassal had the right to make pacts with those weaker than him. He too needed people he could trust and rely on. In return for their help and loyalty, particularly in times of war, he gave them certain benefits.

He could assign part of his fief: a castle; a fortress with a village and fields; a toll road and bridge, or even the right to collect certain taxes.

In fact, the vassal became a feudal lord, creating other vassals beneath him. These were known as *gwass du gwass*, vassals of the vassal, whom we call vavasours. Within the pyramid structure of the feudal system, these vavasours in their turn could concede privileges to other, still weaker vassals.

And the paupers?

Vassals and vavasours were noblemen, or belonged to the clergy. They held their power either because they were proficient with a sword, or because of their calling and their learning. And the poor? Even among them there existed a pyramid structure of social standing.

The craftsmen who worked with iron, leather, wood, wool and other raw materials, making things that the feudal lords really needed, were the most favoured. The baron took them under his protection, giving

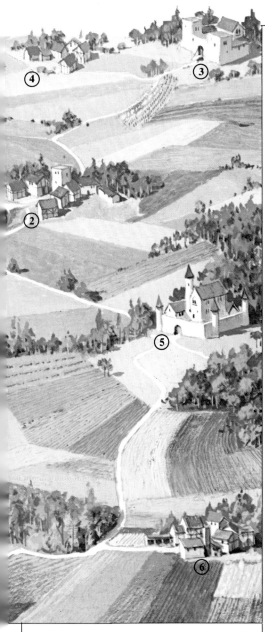

Reconstruction of a fief: some land and villages (2), are held directly by the vassal (1), who has entrusted to vavasours (3), other land and villages (4); these, in their turn, rule over vavasines (5), who control small pieces of land and a few houses (6).

In spite of these heavy charges, it was still an agreement between free men.

Serfs

One cannot say the same of the most humble of all: the serfs of the glebe (soil, or earth). However they did not have such a hard time as is generally believed.

They worked on the land, and were tied to the manor, or freeholding, to which they belonged. If the manor were sold, they too passed to the new owner. They were not, therefore, free men. For the very poor this 'slavery' had certain advantages: security and stability. In an age when peasants were constantly being robbed or deprived of their sole means of subsistence, a system which guaranteed them the privilege of living and working on cultivated land could be considered a distinct advantage.

The standard of living of the serfs varied from manor to manor. The size of the land they were expected to work could be as small as four hectares or as large as thirty. There are records that show that the Abbey of Saint-Germain-des-Prés, in France, had fief over one family of twenty people – two married brothers, one with three children and the other with five, a sister with six children and an unmarried sister. The family had to scratch a living as best they could from their little strip of land as well as work their master's fields.

The services that the serfs performed varied according to technical developments. The invention of the watermill, for instance, released much labour from the boring work of grinding corn by hand, and released more people to work on the land. The exploitation of the land allowed the lords of the manor to appropriate the surplus productive efforts of the peasant families.

The feudal system allowed a relatively small proportion of the population to live in idleness and abundance and to devote their time to fighting and exercising power over their fellow men.

them a house and a workshop. In exchange the craftsmen had to provide each year a certain quantity of goods, and they also had other duties. They were, however, free men.

Many of the farmers who cultivated the feudal lord's fields were also free men. They owned the freehold of the land. The need for protection which was at the root of the feudal system was felt most of all by them, so they bound themselves to a powerful man. They lived in houses around the lord's castle and cultivated his lands in exchange for armed protection. The agreements made between lords and farmers were often very complicated. The farmers worked the lord's land, giving him part of the produce and keeping the rest for themselves and their families. In addition they performed certain duties free: hay-making, helping with the harvest, bridge-building, repairing the castle walls. These obligatory duties were called corvées. Then in one way or another they paid various taxes: for using the lord's bakehouse, for example, or for passing over a bridge that he had built.

Above and right: two miniatures taken from the fifteenth-century Book of Hours, *a magnificently illustrated prayer-book. Painted by the Limbourg brothers, they show the grape harvest and hay-making in the fields around the castle. Centre: helmets and shields with the insignia of feudal lords.*

Europe After Charlemagne

'The Northmen are sacking all the cities they meet in their path and no one can resist them. . . An enormous number of Norse ships is sailing up the Seine. Ruin and destruction are spreading throughout the region. The inhabitants are fleeing . . .' A cry goes up from the courtyard of the monastery at Noirmoutier. The scribe raises his eyes from the scroll: who knows if in later years anyone will read it? He too gathers his few belongings and flees with the rest.

THE AGE OF THE SWORD

Noirmoutier, on the Atlantic coast, was one of the many monasteries during the powerful Carolingian Empire. The words we have just read were inscribed shortly after the Norsemen (men from the North) or Vikings sacked the city of Rouen in 841. For several decades these ferocious Scandinavian warriors had been plundering the North European coasts, breaking down the European unity that Charlemagne had built up.

As well as these attacks on the northern coastline there were savage incursions of barbarian peoples from the East, especially the Hungarians, whose ferocity resembled that of Attila's Huns. However these invasions were not the direct cause of the collapse of the Carolingian Empire. A strong empire, united and well-governed, would have been able to resist the attacks; and this was the case as long as there was an energetic man like Charlemagne holding the reins.

After his death in 814 conflicts and rivalries broke out among his successors. Weakened by these struggles, the Empire, which was already split into a number of counties, dukedoms, fiefs and minor holdings, became a giant jigsaw puzzle in which emperors and kings, feudal lords and powerful men of all kinds appeared and disappeared with great speed. Each one of them tried to obtain for himself as much territory as possible, and the unity created by the Carolingians bent and then broke.

Hard times began for the whole of Europe. Urban civilisation almost disappeared (no town in eastern Europe had more than 20,000 inhabitants). It was the Age of the Sword.

EUROPE AFTER THE TREATY OF VERDUN

The Treaty of Verdun split the Carolingian Empire into three. Charles the Bald obtained the kingdom of the western Franks, which was later to become France. Louis the German got the kingdom of the eastern Franks, which was later to become Germany. Lothar received a band of territories between the other two kingdoms, stretching from the North Sea, through Burgundy, to the Adriatic, including the dukedom of Spoleto.

A few decades later, the divisions which respected national differences were done away with. The largest fiefs, dukedoms and counties became independent, and the feudal lords even assumed the title of king.

(The treaty provided the framework for modern France and Germany. Lothar's portion bisected the Alps and was peopled by races who could not understand each other's speech. It disintegrated almost at once.)

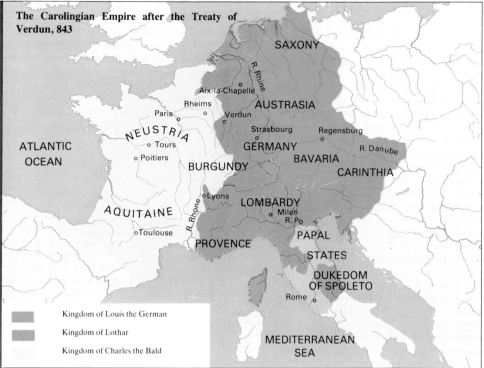

The Carolingian Empire after the Treaty of Verdun, 843

■ Kingdom of Louis the German

■ Kingdom of Lothar

■ Kingdom of Charles the Bald

The decline of the Carolingians

Charlemagne died in 814. He was succeeded by his son, Louis the Pious, whom Charlemagne had been training for some time, placing him on the throne at his side. The name of this devout Carolingian was either Louis or Ludovic, according to whether the French or German version of his name is used.

Despite being well-trained by his wise father, Charlemagne's son made one vital mistake. Following tradition, and his own sense of justice, he divided the Empire among his sons. Lothar, the eldest, took the title of emperor on his father's death. Louis, called the 'German', and Charles, the 'Bald', were jealous of their brother. Conflicts between the brothers over real and assumed rights led to open rebellions against their father.

Louis the Pious died in 840. The struggles between the rival brothers flared up again, even worse than before. Louis the German and Charles the Bald became allies against their common enemy, Lothar, and in 841 beat his troops at the battle of Fontenoy. A year later the two allies met at Strasbourg and made an alliance.

In 843 Louis and Charles persuaded Lothar to accept a treaty. The Treaty of Verdun officially divided the Empire between the three brothers.

Louis and Charles were the real winners. They kept the more compact slices of land for themselves. Lothar received the two capitals, Rome and Aix-la-Chapelle, and with them the imperial title.

In the ninth century the Northmen devastated the coasts of the Atlantic and the Channel.

The birth of two nations

The lands attributed to Lothar by the Treaty of Verdun were an artificial state with no unity: a long band of territories between the two other kingdoms, with frontiers open on both sides. It did not last long. Apart from that, the Verdun agreement established what had already taken place: France on one side, to Charles the Bald; Germany on the other, to Louis the German. They were now two distinct nations, with different destinies and often at war. The bilingual text of the Strasbourg oath recognised this situation: it is the earliest document written in both French and German. The Frankish troops of Charles did not understand the German dialect; the Germanic troops of Louis did not understand French.

However, this division did not solve some problems: in fact, it made them more complex. New struggles between the grandsons of Charlemagne – hereditary questions, revolts, pacts, marriages which brought rich dowries, premature deaths, plots for taking over counties and dukedoms – further split the jigsaw which had once been an empire.

Charles the Bald managed to have himself crowned emperor after the death of his brother. However, he had to pay a very high price. With the famous Quiertzy Capitulary in 877 he had to concede to the most powerful feudal lords the right to pass on their fiefs to their sons. The result was that even if dukedoms and counties continued to belong to the king on paper, they became ever more autonomous and independent. The great feudal lords became more and more like kings of their fiefs and would tolerate no intervention from outsiders regarding the ways in which they chose to run their 'empires'.

MOVEMENT IN EUROPE

The disruption of the Carolingian Empire was one of the principal causes of the 'movement' which took place in Europe between the end of the ninth and the end of the twelfth century. But it was not the only cause. In fact, even on the fringes of the Empire – in places like England and Spain which were outside it, and in Italy where imperial authority was fairly weak – things began to move. For some countries this was the beginning of the discovery of a national identity which was to explode over the following centuries. For others it was chaos which only sorted itself out much later.

However, everywhere in Europe these were troubled and confused decades.

A new dynasty in France

France was racked by the continual bloody incursions of the Northmen; decades later the terrible Hungarians appeared. Charles the Fat reigned, but he did nothing. In 880 the Northmen captured and burnt Nijmegen, and occupied the strongholds of Courtrai and Ghent. A year later they sacked Liège, Aix, Cologne and Bonn. Then in 882 they returned and captured Rheims, where the kings were crowned, and ancient Trier. In 883 they took Amiens and pushed down as far as Paris, where Count Odo, who governed the city, organised a brave resistance for thirteen months. The Northmen only left when Charles the Fat, rather than intervene with an army, paid them a huge sum of silver and allowed them passage up the Seine to winter in Burgundy. With the arrival of spring they sacked it. Odo, the Count of Paris, who followed in the footsteps of his father, Robert the Strong, didn't offer the other cheek to the invaders but dealt them a

decisive defeat. With Charles the Fat deposed, Odo was named *Rex Francorum*, King of France, by the frightened and admiring lords.

A France which was no longer great, since the great fiefs – Champagne, Aquitaine, Gascony, Toulouse, Gothia, Catalonia, Brittany, Normandy, Flanders – had all become independent.

For another century the Northmen's raids continued, and the lords of Paris resisted strenuously. They were not always kings (that depended on election by the great lords), but they were always highly esteemed. With arms and money, one of Odo's grandsons took possession of a vast amount of land, from Normandy to the Seine and the Loire. Hugh the Great was richer and more powerful than the king he paid homage to. It was not surprising that his son, Hugh Capet, was unanimously elected king of France in 987. Thus began the dynasty that was to remain in power for another 800 years.

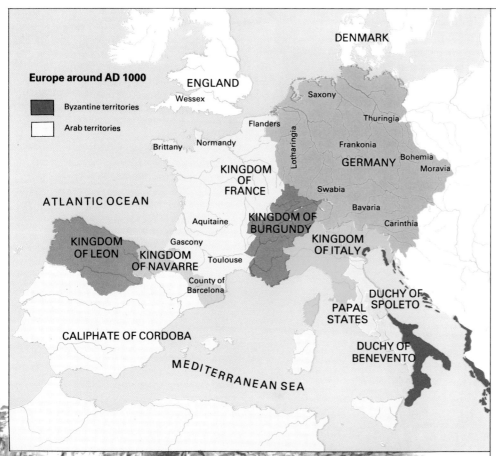

Europe around AD 1000

- ■ Byzantine territories
- □ Arab territories

DENMARK

ENGLAND
Wessex

Saxony

Thuringia

Flanders

Normandy

Brittany

Lotharingia

Frankonia

GERMANY

Bohemia

Moravia

KINGDOM OF FRANCE

ATLANTIC OCEAN

Swabia

Aquitaine

KINGDOM OF BURGUNDY

Bavaria

Carinthia

KINGDOM OF LEON

Gascony

KINGDOM OF NAVARRE

Toulouse

KINGDOM OF ITALY

County of Barcelona

PAPAL STATES

DUCHY OF SPOLETO

CALIPHATE OF CORDOBA

DUCHY OF BENEVENTO

MEDITERRANEAN SEA

Rebirth of the Empire in Germany

Fiefs were also set up in the lands allotted to Louis the German: the powerful dukedoms of Saxony, Thuringia, Bavaria, Swabia, Lotharingia (Lorraine) and Franconia. A strong leader was also chosen here: the Duke of Saxony, called 'the Fowler' because of his passion for hunting with birds. He was elected King Henry I in 919. He routed the Slavs, fortified the borders of Germany with castles, and formed a magnificent body of cavalry to fight off the invasions of the Hungarians. His son, Otto the Great, was also called the Charlemagne of Germany. In 996, at the age of twenty-four, he was elected king. In the next thirty-seven years he defeated many great feudal lords who rebelled. Their fiefs went to members of his own family. Otto soundly defeated the Hungarians and the Slavs in two battles on the river Lech in 955. In the year 962 Otto the Great was crowned Emperor of the Holy Roman Empire at Rome. It seemed that the crown of Charlemagne, which for decades had been dragged in the dust, had finally been placed on the right head. The Carolingian Empire was reborn with the name of the Holy Roman Empire, this time set up by the German people.

England against the Danes

The Romans abandoned England in about AD 400. Half a century later the rulers of England were sea-faring barbarians: Jutes, Angles and Saxons. The numerous kingdoms fought bitterly among themselves and on several occasions were attacked by Vikings.

Viking raiders plagued England for many years from 793 when they pillaged the monastery at Lindisfarne. In 866 the Vikings began their systematic conquest of England, and the country came to be governed by Danes (a Danelaw). However in 871 a twenty-three-year-old man came to the throne of Wessex, a kingdom which extended from Land's End to the North Sea. The West Saxons had always been a stubborn people, offering brave resistance to the Danish invaders. The new king, Alfred, defeated the Danes at the Battle of Edington in 878 and forced them to accept a partition of the country along the imaginary line that ran from London to Chester. Alfred was a man of culture as well as being a great warrior. He delighted in songs and literature, cared about education and learning, and was a concerned law-giver. In driving the Danes out of Wessex he secured the survival of Anglo-Saxon civilisation and laid the foundations of a national state of Britain.

The kings and lords of the Middle Ages loved to go hunting. It was both an amusement and an exercise to keep them fit for war. Here we see King Henry I of Saxony hunting wild boar.

ITALY, A FIEF OF THE GERMANIC EMPIRE

Bitter fighting broke out in Italy with the fall of the Carolingian Empire. Everyone seemed to have legitimate rights over the others. Naturally the rights of the Church were untouchable; and the Byzantine Empire, though it was far off and uninterested, was still powerful. The lords fought over the ancient dukedoms of the central southern Langobards, which had been conquered by the Franks, and over the hereditary lands of the French sovereigns, whether they were legitimate or not. A troublesome and confused period began in Italy where the Langobards had established themselves from Scandinavia in the seventh century. After Charlemagne's death, the Langobard rulers of Tuscany and Spoleto became increasingly independent.

A coin from the reign of Berengario I

A feudal kingdom

Berengario, Marquis of Friuli, was on his mother's side a nephew of Louis the Pious, Charlemagne's son. With the ending of the direct line of Carolingians, who had a more legitimate right to the throne of Italy? Guido of Spoleto, the heir to the Langobard dukedoms, had different ideas. He was helped by the Pope, who gave him and his son Lamberto not only the title of King of Italy, but also the imperial crown. The Pope, it should be said, was forced to do this by the Spoletines.

Other legitimate Carolingian heirs were also pretenders to the title. A new Pope was an enemy of the Spoletines, so another legitimate Carolingian king was elected: Arnolfo di Carinzia. When he was deposed Berengario was elected in his place. After Berengario came Louis of Provence, who was deposed by Rudolf of Burgundy. Meanwhile the powerful men of Rome ruled as lords in their own right, and even elected their own popes.

Next came Hugh of Provence, his bastard son Albario, his son Hugh, and finally Berengario II, Marquis of Ivrea . . . It is not hard to imagine just what a confused state Italy was in between 888 and 950.

Berengario held Lothar's widow a captive as he considered her a threat to his position. She appealed for help to Otto, son of Henry the Fowler, who had driven the Magyars out of Germany.

The 'German Charlemagne', Otto I, tried to sort things out. He swept into Italy declaring that the Holy Roman Empire of the Germanic nation was born. He had himself crowned by the Pope, and reduced Italy to the state of a fief of the German Empire.

Italy had never been so subjected to the will of others as in those times. However . . . here and there along the coast little flames of liberty were being lit.

The seafaring cities

New cities, or cities which had once been great and were now decayed, were coming to life. Sea trade was rediscovered; ships were put out to sea. At first these were simply large rowing boats, used to transport salt, dry fish and other coastal products inland along the rivers. They brought back wood, grain, skins and minerals and sold them to the rich Byzantine cities who were willing to pay well for them.

First Ravenna, then Ancona and Bari were established. As the seafarers grew bolder they pushed out from the Mediterranean to Northern Africa, and even as far as Byzantium. Venice, Genoa, Amalfi, Pisa – as well as other coastal cities – were founded at this time. These new cities later led to the rebirth of Italy, and brought about new, more democratic ways of living.

Thanks to sea trade, Venice grew from the miserable group of huts on the lagoon, as we see here, to become a great marine power.

The Northmen

In a Viking village at the end of a fjord the women are busy with domestic tasks; the men are at work.

Some have already put out to sea, some are making preparations and others are repairing a ship ready to leave.

From these Scandinavian coasts the Northmen set out, over a period from the eighth to the eleventh centuries. Spurred on by their love of adventure and of the unknown, they crossed the seas to discover new lands, conquer territories and found kingdoms on far distant shores.

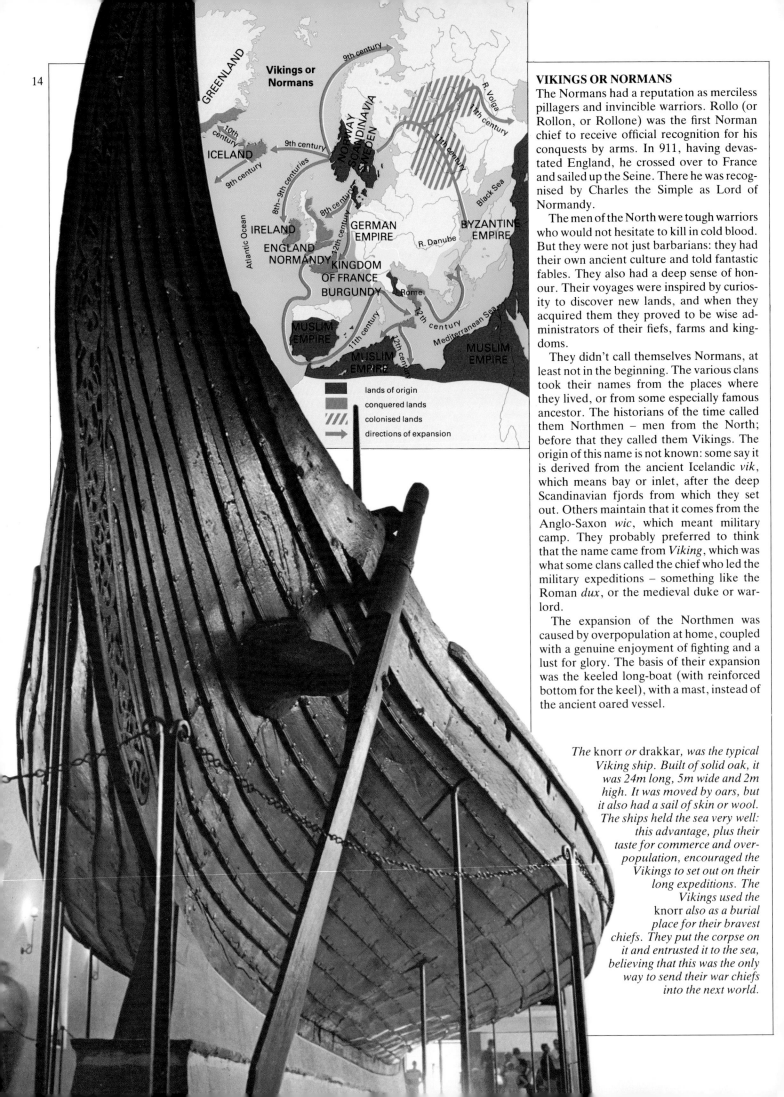

14

Vikings or Normans

lands of origin
conquered lands
colonised lands
directions of expansion

GREENLAND

ICELAND
9th century
10th century
8th-9th centuries
9th century

IRELAND
ENGLAND
NORMANDY

Atlantic Ocean

NORWAY
SCANDINAVIA
SWEDEN

9th century
8th century
12th century

GERMAN
EMPIRE

R. Danube

KINGDOM
OF FRANCE
BURGUNDY

Rome

11th century
12th century
12th century

MUSLIM
EMPIRE

MUSLIM
EMPIRE

R. Volga
11th century
11th century

Black Sea

BYZANTINE
EMPIRE

Mediterranean Sea

MUSLIM
EMPIRE

VIKINGS OR NORMANS

The Normans had a reputation as merciless pillagers and invincible warriors. Rollo (or Rollon, or Rollone) was the first Norman chief to receive official recognition for his conquests by arms. In 911, having devastated England, he crossed over to France and sailed up the Seine. There he was recognised by Charles the Simple as Lord of Normandy.

The men of the North were tough warriors who would not hesitate to kill in cold blood. But they were not just barbarians: they had their own ancient culture and told fantastic fables. They also had a deep sense of honour. Their voyages were inspired by curiosity to discover new lands, and when they acquired them they proved to be wise administrators of their fiefs, farms and kingdoms.

They didn't call themselves Normans, at least not in the beginning. The various clans took their names from the places where they lived, or from some especially famous ancestor. The historians of the time called them Northmen – men from the North; before that they called them Vikings. The origin of this name is not known: some say it is derived from the ancient Icelandic *vik*, which means bay or inlet, after the deep Scandinavian fjords from which they set out. Others maintain that it comes from the Anglo-Saxon *wic*, which meant military camp. They probably preferred to think that the name came from *Viking*, which was what some clans called the chief who led the military expeditions – something like the Roman *dux*, or the medieval duke or warlord.

The expansion of the Northmen was caused by overpopulation at home, coupled with a genuine enjoyment of fighting and a lust for glory. The basis of their expansion was the keeled long-boat (with reinforced bottom for the keel), with a mast, instead of the ancient oared vessel.

The knorr *or* drakkar, *was the typical Viking ship. Built of solid oak, it was 24m long, 5m wide and 2m high. It was moved by oars, but it also had a sail of skin or wool. The ships held the sea very well: this advantage, plus their taste for commerce and overpopulation, encouraged the Vikings to set out on their long expeditions. The Vikings used the* knorr *also as a burial place for their bravest chiefs. They put the corpse on it and entrusted it to the sea, believing that this was the only way to send their war chiefs into the next world.*

From the deep Scandinavian fjords . . .

The Vikings came from Scandinavia, modern Denmark, Sweden, Norway and part of Finland. They placed their villages on the shores of deep fjords, where the lean fields allowed them to farm and raise animals. Meat, milk, butter, cheese, cereals (wheat in milder areas; barley and oats elsewhere), vegetables (cabbages and peas), apples and pears made up their basic diet. The poverty of their lands, and the increase in population, probably led them to seek their fortune elsewhere. The directions of Viking expansion are shown on the map. Expeditions were usually made by one or more united clans. Later on (the beginning of their expansion dates back to 793), at the time of the decline of the Carolingians, entire Scandinavian tribes took part in military expeditions. These led to the social and political transformation of England, Holland, Northern France and Ireland.

Longships

The basic instrument of Viking expansion was the *knorr*, the military longship. Low in the water, tapered, supple – it was affectionately nicknamed by the Vikings 'the warhorse of the waves'. But those who saw it appear on the horizon called it *drakkar* or *drakken*, meaning dragon, because the prow often ended in a dragon's head. The *knorrs* were propelled by long oars, worked by sailor-warriors, and by a large square sail. The wide shallow keel meant that the ships could ascend rivers to attack and destroy inland towns.

Village life

The Vikings lived in small villages. The houses were usually made of wood, the roofs covered with straw or earth.

The buildings were often up to thirty metres long, and consisted of a kitchen, and a few small nooks enclosed by curtains which they used as bedrooms. The toilets, stables, wood store and furnace for working metals were all outside. Viking society was divided into classes. A chief, or king, led the clan in war. But the rest of the time important decisions were taken by the *thing* – an assembly of free men. Larger assemblies of people from much wider areas, the first of which took place in 930, were called *al thing*.

The free men were the *jarls*, rich farmers who formed the nucleus of Viking armies; and below them the *karls*, smallholders who worked their own land.

At the bottom of society were the slaves, or *thralls*, prisoners-of-war or debtors reduced to servitude for not paying their debts. Their masters had the power of life or death over them.

Their gods

Unike the Greeks and the Romans who had treated their gods as superior beings that should be served, the Vikings treated theirs as friends and allies in the great adventures of life. If a Viking was brave and fortunate enough to die in battle he would be allowed to enter the great halls of Valhalla where all heroes killed in combat spent their days in fights and feasting. The Northmen knew too much about the wildness of nature and the furious passions of man to ask more from

life than life could give. Their literature stands out for its freedom from sentiment and gives a picture of a society that was aristocratic and anarchic, violent and cruel but ennobled by a proud acceptance of inevitable fate.

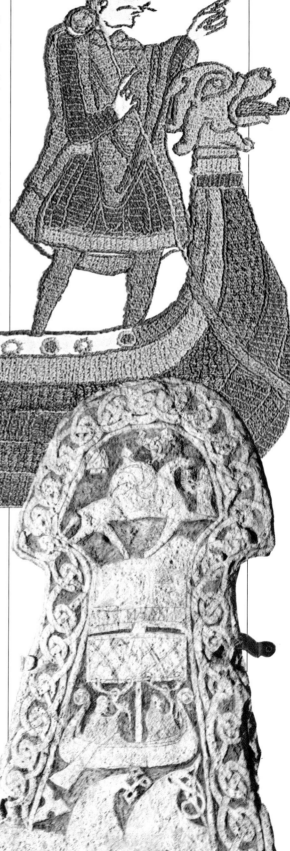

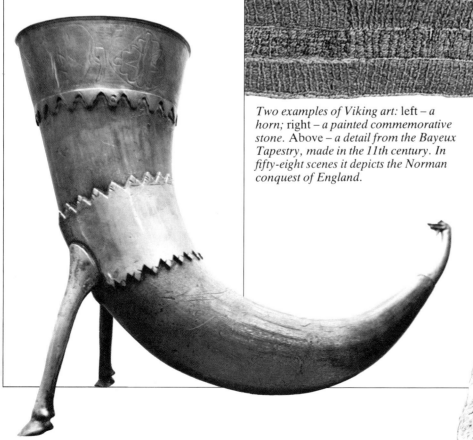

Two examples of Viking art: left – *a horn;* right – *a painted commemorative stone.* Above – *a detail from the Bayeux Tapestry, made in the 11th century. In fifty-eight scenes it depicts the Norman conquest of England.*

CONQUERING FIEFS AND KINGDOMS

Although Vikings had been terrorising the coasts of Northern Europe for thirty years or more, the beginning of their expansion dates from 793, when various clans joined together to attack and plunder the monastery of Lindisfarne on the north-east coast of England. In 795, other Vikings took possession in Ireland.

These first conquests opened the way for expeditions on a greater scale. Not knowing what to call them, their victims gave them the name of the 'Men from the North', or Northmen.

The terror of Europe

As long as Western Europe had an effective defence, represented by the army of Charlemagne, the Vikings suffered heavy defeats. But when the defence of the borders was abandoned, because the sons and grandsons of Charlemagne were too busy fighting each other, the Northmen became the plague of Northern Europe.

The *knorrs*, full of Viking warriors, would suddenly be sighted by the inhabitants of a town or village. Many abandoned their possessions and tried to flee before the murderous soldiers cut them down with their long swords and axes. The villages were plundered and then burned to the ground.

In this way the Vikings had conquered, by 830, most of Ireland, north-east England and Holland. They had even reached as far as the coasts of Spain and into the Mediterranean; and Vikings from Sweden had penetrated into the heart of Russia, setting up a kingdom with the capital city at Kiev.

In the far North, Vikings from Norway colonised Iceland in 874, Greenland in 982, and probably reached North America at the beginning of the eleventh century.

Vikings from Denmark established a kingdom in England; and as we have already seen, Rollo and his men occupied the land which later became Normandy. Charles the Simple practically invited them to occupy what they already possessed: he made Rollo a duke and his vassal. The result of this was, first, Rollo and his men bravely defended Northern France from further Viking aggression; and, second, the Normans rapidly adapted to French habits and became the new protagonists of European history. The latter had not been part of Charles the Simple's plan.

On the left and the far right are details of a scene from the Bayeux Tapestry, showing Norman knights attacking King Harold's men at the Battle of Hastings in 1066.
In the centre: the handle of a Viking sword, made of silver and iron and decorated with stylised animals.
Behind: Rochester Castle, built in the twelfth century. After conquering a country the Normans then had to defend it against attacks from other Vikings. This is why they left behind numerous castles in England, Normandy and Southern Italy.

The Norman kingdom in England

The Normans may have been merciless warriors, but they were not stupid barbarians. In fact they proved to be the most acute and energetic of all the powerful peoples of that tormented period. In Normandy they were soon converted from paganism to catholicism, and adopted French as their language, learning civil customs without losing their military strength. Normandy was organised into a strong and well-administered state. However, the Normans did not lose their taste for conquest.

In the eleventh century, the English sovereign Edward the Confessor died without leaving a son. He named as his successor William of Normandy, a descendant of Rollo. But the Saxon lords elected instead one of their own number, Harold, the king's brother-in-law and the most powerful man in England.

William assembled an army and crossed the Channel to fight Harold at the Battle of Hastings in 1066. The Normans won the battle and Harold, shot in the eye with an arrow, died on the battlefield. William the Conqueror was crowned King at Westminster in October of that year.

The Normans soon established a well-organised state, as they had done in Normandy. The French language, which was brought in by the conquerors, was mixed with the Anglo-Saxon language to become the modern English.

By the time William died in 1087 England was the most powerful country in Western Europe.

The Normans in Italy

About the middle of the ninth century the Vikings began to penetrate Southern Europe: Spain and Portugal in 844; Italy in 859. Later, in the tenth and eleventh centuries, they were followed by Normans from France and England. The Norman laws, under which the eldest son inherited everything, meant that younger sons had to go elsewhere to seek their fortune. They became adventurers; mercenaries who fought for whoever paid them most.

One of them was particularly lucky. He was Rainulf Drengot, who in 1027 gained the title of Count of Aversa, near Naples. But the real fortunes of the Normans in Italy began with the Hauteville (or Altavilla) brothers. They were the eleven sons of a dispossessed nobleman who sold his services as a soldier to the highest bidder.

. . . and in Sicily

The oldest of the Hauteville brothers, William – nicknamed the 'Iron Arm' – was given the county of Melfi, in Apulia, in 1043. The next brother, Robert – called 'Guis-card', the sharp – succeeded him as head of the band of Normans who plundered Southern Italy. The Pope gave him the dukedom of Calabria in Apulia in exchange for his allegiance.

A third brother, Roger, took over Sicily, expelling the Moors (the Muslims who had governed it fairly well) with the approval of the Pope. Robert the Guiscard died without heir and Roger's son. Roger II, inherited all the Italo-Norman possessions. They were worthy of a king; and in 1130 the Pope crowned Roger II at Palermo – King of Sicily, and Duke of Calabria and Apulia.

England, Normandy, Southern Italy and Russia had been conquered by the Vikings: the 'Men from the North' who, two centuries before, had left their fjords because of the famine. They could not have imagined they would have such success!

The scene in the lands from whence they had sailed so long ago was completely different. There the Viking aristocracy all but died out in a series of useless and stupid civil wars, and by the thirteenth century Scandinavia was populated by a rude, illiterate peasantry scratching a bare living from the barren soil of the North lands.

18

At the time of Charlemagne an Arab caliph wrote: 'The Christians of the Mediterranean would no longer be capable of making even a plank float.'

This scornful remark referred to the decline in maritime trade in Western Europe. However, after AD 1000 several Italian and French cities, starting with Marseilles, began

launching ships again. With the revival of European economy these cities quickly flourished and became prosperous once more and paved the way for the eventual expansion of European culture.

Europe AD 1000

THE REBIRTH OF EUROPEAN ECONOMY

Around AD 1000 the economy of Western Europe revived and this led to a general improvement in living standards and to a new way of thinking. As we shall see, there were several reasons for this. Some improvements were brought about by different ways of working; others were influenced by social and political changes.

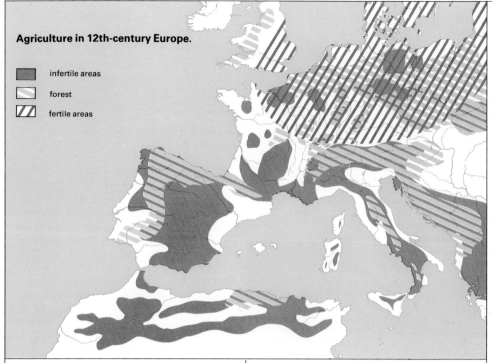

Agriculture in 12th-century Europe.

- infertile areas
- forest
- fertile areas

These were the men and women who brought about the economic and social revival in Europe.

The conquest of new lands

In AD 1000 Europe was made up of thousands of feudal courts, successors of the Carolingian noblemen; or, in Southern Europe, the Romans. The farms and fields around the lord's castle provided food and work for a few dozen families. The peasants cultivated the lands of the feudal lord and kept most of the harvest in return for certain obligatory duties.

When the number of people needing food increased, the system began to change. With or without the consent of the feudal lord, groups of peasants began to move into new, uncultivated lands. These pioneers chopped down the ancient forests, cleared the ground and created grazing land and fields. They dug canals in swampy places and diverted the excess water in dry areas. At the bottom of valleys they ploughed up the heavy soil and planted grain. The hill slopes were planted with vines.

As you can see on the map, some regions were completely transformed in this way. Groups of peasants from Holland chopped down the forests and dug up the land in the German wastelands of Thuringia and Saxony. The German peasants, protected by armed soldiers and helped by monks, moved over the river Oder and pushed into the endless plains that stretched away to Russia.

In England a vast forest ran up the west of the country but the south-east was fertile and well cultivated.

In France it was in Normandy, the Massif Central, the slopes of the Pyrenees and in Burgundy that the forests were cleared. In Italy the peasants, helped by the experience of the Benedictine monks, reclaimed the swampy plain of the river Po. It was in this way that the face of Europe began to be fashioned by the hand of man.

It was the same spirit that, centuries later, caused men and women to leave their native countries and sail across the seas to the Americas and, later, to Australia and Africa where they also changed the physical appearance of these continents and tried to impose European culture on the native peoples there.

The increase in population

Towards the end of the tenth century the emperors of the Germanic Holy Roman Empire had managed to re-establish a certain amount of law and order in imperial territories. Their successors continued in the same way, and their example was followed by the kings of the various parts of Europe. The Church, too, worked tirelessly for peace, and had a positive influence on the revival of economic activity.

To live in peace meant to work in peace: to put down roots and raise a family. During this period of relative peace, the population increased in all European countries.

The improvement in living conditions reduced infant mortality. The people ate badly, but they all had food. A family of five or six children was common. The average life expectancy was about forty-five years.

The disappearance of invading armies and the introduction of a few basic hygienic standards meant that the spread of epidemics was controlled. Living-quarters were separated from the animal stalls; ditches were dug for the removal of waste; the rough cotton or hemp shirts were washed occasionally; sometimes the people even took a bath! Diseases which had previously killed many people, particularly children, became less frequent.

More hands to till the soil; more sharp minds for commerce

The children who were born, and survived in greater numbers, meant more mouths to feed. But when they grew up there were more hands to till the soil: to chop down the forests and transform the wilderness of Europe into a cultivated and productive garden.

Not all of them were destined to work on the land. Among them were future warriors, adventurers who took part in the Crusades and merchants who traded their goods round the country, despite the danger from brigands.

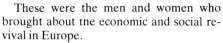

At the end of the eleventh century Marseilles became a busy maritime city. On the quay porters are loading and unloading merchandise; spices, carpets, bales of cloth, and so on. Warships guard the mouth of the port: they protected the trading vessels against attacks from pirates. The French and Italian ports soon re-established themselves as important commercial centres.

A REAWAKENING AFTER THE 'GREAT FEAR'

'1000 and no more than 1000.' This obscure prophecy from the Biblical Book of Revelation was interpreted as meaning that on 31st December 999 the world would come to an end. Panic spread. With fiery words preachers invited sinners to repent, and churches and chapels were built everywhere.

When the sun rose on the morning of 1st January in the year 1000 and nothing apocalyptic happened, the people felt a new hope and a new faith springing up in their hearts.

The will to survive and rebuild was uppermost.

The building of hundreds of churches and magnificent cathedrals was an affirmation of the general reawakening which swept through Europe.

The circulation of money

The new economic well-being changed the relationship between the feudal lords and the peasants who cultivated their lands. The lords now preferred money in exchange: this was called quit-rent. This arrangement also suited the peasants. By selling at the market any produce the family did not need, they obtained money to pay the rent of their farm and no longer had any other obligations to the lord.

The feudal lords used the money to pay for any services or work they wanted done, such as repairs to the castle, which before had been done unwillingly by the serfs. Money began to circulate, and as a result commerce developed rapidly.

Rebirth of the towns and cities

We said that the peasants sold their goods: but where, to whom, and in what way? In Europe, after the fall of the Roman Empire, city life became more and more stagnant until it almost died out. The cities lost their importance because life was centred in the countryside. Only a few large ones continued to survive, and these were all outside Western Europe: Constantinople, Baghdad, Cairo, Cordova, Palermo, Seville. . . After AD 1000 the ancient cities founded by the Romans came to life again and their populations increased. New towns and cities also sprang up. All of them gradually won a certain independence and were given rights.

In central and south-west France the settlements, built by the peasants who cleared the land, consisted of low houses laid out on a regular pattern around a church and a town square. A second square, often behind the church, became a marketplace. These *bastides* or *villeneuves* were enclosed by high walls of rectangular shape.

In Germany settlements sprang up around a fortress, or *burg*. The word *burg* appears in the name of many towns. A church and some houses were built near the fortress, and these became the nucleus of the new city, which slowly spread to new quarters, each divided up by roads and squares.

In England, in the twelfth and thirteenth centuries, the kings took an active role in creating and planning towns. In 1297, Edward I held a meeting of town planners at Harwich and by that time more than 120 towns had been 'planned', including Richmond and Bury St Edmunds. Richard I had been responsible for founding Portsmouth and his brother John for founding Liverpool. These planned towns were built on a chequerboard pattern where possible, although the slope of the land or the course of a river would have some bearing on what a town would look like.

Left: façade of the church of St Michael in Pavia, Northern Italy, founded by the Langobards or Lombards. It was rebuilt at the beginning of the twelfth century on the tide of religious fervour which swept through Europe after AD 1000.
Right: merchants in front of Bruges castle.

THE CITY OF BRUGES

This is how the Flemish city of Bruges, later an important port and centre for the development of trade, got its name: 'Merchants selling expensive wares to satisfy the needs of the inhabitants of the castle gathered near the entrance, in front of the drawbridge. Inns, and then hostels were set up to provide food and shelter for the merchants. Then houses were built nearby for those who couldn't be accommodated at the castle. When asked for directions they said: "We're going to the bridge".'

The word brugg *means bridge, and this is where the name of the city originated.*

The merchants

Economic expansion gradually changed Europe from a system of feudal courts to a network of 'feudal cities'. As new cities were built, or ancient ones were repopulated, the people were divided into two distinct categories. The farmers, and the peasants who lived on the land of the feudal lords, were by far the most numerous. But it was the people who lived in the towns whose lives changed most. They were called burghers – that is, inhabitants of a *burg* or *burgh* – and were divided into craftsmen and merchants.

The craftsmen worked in shops in the city, producing goods not only for their own use, or for a small group of people (as was the case with the blacksmith and carpenter of the feudal courts), but also to sell for money. For this reason they were always striving to improve their wares, choosing raw materials carefully and trying new ways of producing original articles. The craftsmen joined together in companies, or associations, to limit the competition to those in the same city.

The merchants didn't produce anything themselves, but earned money through the work of others. They acted as intermediaries between producers and customers, buying from one and selling to the other, often in another city. Naturally they kept a certain amount of profit for themselves, and sometimes this was very high.

Men without scruples . . .

In fact merchants were not new characters in medieval life: they were often present in feudal courts. They usually came from the Eastern Empire, or from the Islamic countries, and they offered precious goods – cloth, perfumes, jewels – that only the rich lords could buy.

But now the merchants became very important, even outside rich circles. They were the link that connected the countryside to the cities, and all the goods passed through them.

Not everybody liked these people who earned money without doing anything productive with their hands.

. . . or necessary to society?

Others thought differently. Even if they realised that the average merchant was more interested in money than in moral scruples, they still considered that they were necessary to society.

However they were judged, the merchants encouraged money to circulate, which led to a whole series of other activities. This had two effects: an increase in the prosperity of the nation and the stimulation of the new European economy to take on more ambitious enterprises.

The work of the pioneering peasants, the craftsmen of the towns, and of the merchants, helped Europe to the position of economic power that it still occupies today.

22

'There is no magic in mechanical arts. One day man will build machines for navigation . . . wagons that move with incredible speed but do not need animals . . . flying machines with artificial wings like those of a bird, that a man can sit comfortably inside . . . machines for raising and lowering incredibly heavy weights . . . machines for descending to the depths of the sea with no danger of dying . . . bridges suspended over water without pillars or arches.' These words were written by Roger Bacon in the thirteenth century. What incredible foresight he had!

AN UNJUSTLY CRITICISED ERA

For a long time the Middle Ages were considered a 'dead' period of scientific development and technological progress. A prophet of the future like Roger Bacon, who lived from 1214 to 1292, was an exception. But now we realise that the five centuries between AD 1000 and 1500 were in fact a time of considerable change. There were no spectacular discoveries or inventions of the kind that open up new horizons for mankind – like, for example, the invention of the steam engine, the discovery of electricity, or atomic energy, or space technology – but fundamental improvements in daily life and work transformed the existence of the ordinary people.

We will look now at the most significant of these innovations, starting with the most basic.

Progress in the agricultural world

In the previous chapter we talked about the economic revival that took place in Europe after the year AD 1000. An important factor in this 'rebirth' was that farmers were now able to produce more than they needed just to keep their own families alive. The excess goods could be sold or exchanged for other things at the markets and fairs, giving an increased impetus to commerce and, as a result, to craftsmen and to industry.

A number of technological innovations of this time were particularly relevant to agriculture, and played an important part in the general increase in production.

A new type of plough

Ancient civilisations were developed mainly in the warm areas around the Mediterranean, where the land was dry and the soil light and crumbly. The main problem for the farmers was to keep any dampness in the ground for as long as possible. They used a light plough without wheels: in fact, it was just a sort of strong peg that dug into the ground. If they had dug too deeply the earth would have been exposed to the heat of the sun, causing it to dry out. They ploughed the fields in parallel furrows; then ploughed it a second time the other way to break up the clods.

This procedure, ideal for the Mediterranean climate, was not at all suitable for Northern Europe. The ground was very damp and heavy, and the excessive mois-

Technology in the Middle Ages

ture damaged the roots of the small plants.

After a great deal of experimentation a new type of plough was adopted, and it is still in use today. This plough was heavier than the Mediterranean one, and it had wheels, which made it easier to pull. In front of the ploughshare there was a long vertical iron blade which made the first cut into the heavy ground. The ploughshare was made from iron, and this turned over the clods of earth. It ended in a mouldboard which pushed the earth to the left and right of the furrow.

In this way a long mound of earth was formed between two parallel furrows. This was very useful. When the season was too dry, the grain grew in the furrows, which retained the moisture. When the weather was wet it grew on the mounds, while the excess water drained into the furrows.

Agriculture at this time was still the concern of tenant farmers whose lands did not form compact blocks, but consisted of a number of narrow strips scattered all over the manor. The reason for this was to prevent one farmer having all the good land and another infertile land. The strip system allowed the land to be shared fairly among all the farmers.

The strips were open so that cattle could go on to them after each harvest, eat what they could find and enrich the soil with their manure. The strips were long and narrow so that the heavy plough would not have to turn too often.

The plough did its job rapidly but needed as many as eight horses to pull it. It was usual, therefore, for ploughing to be done communally, by harnessing together the horses of several tenants.

This arrangement had several advantages, but the absence of hedges, and the fact that the land could revert to the lord of the manor on the death of the tenant, discouraged efforts to improve the land and stifled individual initiative.

More efficient harnessing
From the time that horses were domesticated men knew that they were faster and stronger than the ox. But they hardly ever used them in the fields because there was no harness suitable for heavy work.

The traditional harness of the time consisted of a collar tied loosely round the horse's neck (A). The more the horse pulled, the tighter the collar became, making it difficult for the animal to breathe.

In the early Middle Ages the 'necklace'

Thanks to numerous technological improvements, such as the new type of plough and the use of horses to pull it, it was possible to make the heavy North European soil fertile. This led to a significant increase in agricultural production.

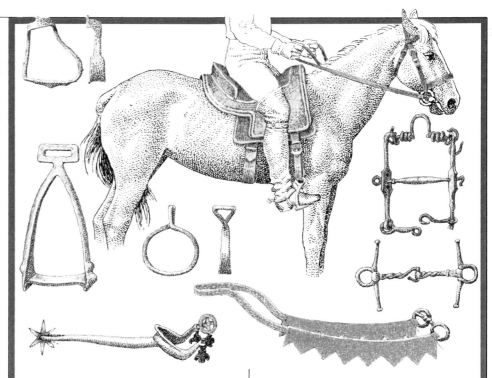

SHOES, STIRRUPS AND SADDLES
In Mediterranean and African climates horses' hooves wore down very little. Special shoes or leather sandals called hipposandals were sufficient to protect them. But in the damp climate of central and north Europe, where the ground was often very heavy, the hooves wore down quickly. Shoeing – the practice of strengthening the hoof with shaped iron – was one of the inventions of the Middle Ages that helped to make the horse indispensable to man. It was not the only one.

The curved saddle made riding easier, giving more stability in the backwards and forwards movement. This was particularly important in battle.

The stirrup was probably introduced by barbarian invaders from the East. One was joined to the saddle on each side, giving the rider somewhere firm to put his feet, and ensuring greater stability in a sideways direction. This enabled a soldier to hold a heavy lance with two hands; and, by rising up in his stirrups, he could fight with a sword from a higher and more favourable position.

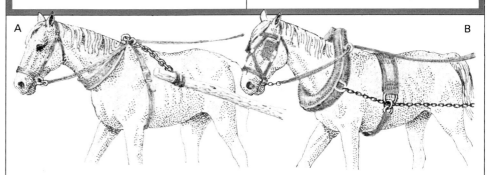

collar was invented. This stiff, padded collar rested on the horse's shoulders and did not restrict its breathing (B). Another improvement was made by changing the position of the horses in a team. In ancient times two, four, or even six horses were harnessed side by side in front of a wagon. The strength of the animals was under-used as it was not concentrated in the right place. In the Middle Ages the traditional system was improved by putting one horse in front of another in a line, or pairs of horses in lines. This arrangement exercised a much greater force (C).

THE ENERGY PROBLEM

The industrialised world of the twentieth century is faced with a serious problem: energy. Until a few years ago oil seemed as if it would satisfy the ever increasing need. But recently people have begun to appreciate the need to conserve our oil supplies, as they are in danger of running out. It is therefore important to find an alternative source of energy.

Expensive research projects have been set up to find new sources of energy. As more reports are published, one fact seems clear, it is to the freely available natural energy sources that twentieth-century man will have to return.

A similar problem existed around the eleventh century. At that time energy was created by man and his animals. The increase in economic activity highlighted the need for new sources of energy. The problem was brilliantly resolved.

Energy from water

In ancient empires there were plenty of slaves, so the production of energy was never a problem. But in the Middle Ages the decline of slavery, together with the spread of new technological developments, led people to rediscover and expand an invention first made centuries before: the watermill.

The earliest watermills were used in the Middle East, in Greece, and by the Romans, as early as 1000 BC. Four centuries later, we are told by an historian of the time, they existed on a tributary of the river Moselle.

The use of the watermill spread rapidly: first in Germany in the eighth century; then, a century later, in France and England; and then in Ireland, Denmark and Iceland.

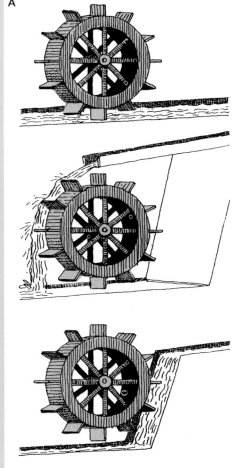

A

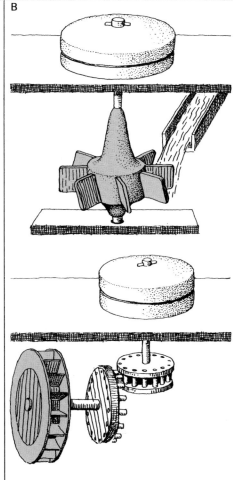

B

THE WATERMILL

As you can see above, the principle of a watermill is quite simple. The force of the running water, or of water falling from above, causes a large wheel to turn (A). The cogs transmit this constant movement to a millstone. This rotates on a fixed stone and grinds the grain into flour (B).

Using this basic principle much more complicated machines were developed (C, D).

These were used for all kinds of different purposes: fulling cloth; pressing apples for cider or grapes for wine, and so on.

The miller's wheel

The earliest and most widespread use of the watermill was for grinding corn and other cereals. At first the introduction of the mill led to peasant uprisings, which were often repressed rather violently with great loss of blood. As soon as the feudal lords recognised the usefulness of the mill, they made it obligatory to grind all grain in their mills on payment of a fee. Anyone caught grinding it by hand was punished.

Gradually the mill became more common, and the miller's house became the focal point of village life.

Uses of the hydraulic wheel

When a rotating shaft was joined to the hub of an hydraulic wheel, a chain of buckets connected to the shaft could raise water from a well to irrigate dry, unproductive land (A). The same process could be used for draining flooded mineshafts, bringing old abandoned mines back into use.

In (B) we can see another strange application of hydraulic energy. The workman is making wire. The metal, roughly entwined, is forced through a small hole. The workman sits on a swing, holding a pair of strong pliers in his hands. With these he grasps the end of the wire as it comes through the hole. As the swing is attached to a winch moved by the hydraulic wheel, the workman swings backwards and forwards. On the backward movement the wire is pulled to the correct size.

This is an example of another important step forward – transforming the circular movement of the hydraulic wheel into a backwards and forwards motion.

The circular movement could also be turned into a rectilinear movement in an up and down direction. The rotating shaft connected to the hub of the hydraulic wheel had protuberances. When the cam shaft was turned the protuberances caught on another

part of the machine, thus raising or lowering the tool to do the work.

This invention had many applications in craftwork and industry. In the first example (C), the large, heavy hammers rise and fall, crushing the minerals used in a foundry. In (D) the cam shaft works a heavy mallet which forges fused iron, removing the waste, to transform it into steel.

At this time, steel was a luxury product, used in the manufacture of swords and other arms, carried out almost exclusively in Spain where the Catalonian forge was developed. The great leap forward in steel production came in 1340 with the development of the Stuckhofen *(an early form of blast furnace) in Germany. This enabled the producer to control the steel-making process more efficiently.*

Energy from wind

Another source of energy was also exploited during the Middle Ages: the wind. Windmills became popular in regions that lacked water, but where there was plenty of wind. Like the waterwheel, windmills had been around for a long time, particularly in Asia. The principle of the windmill and its application were more or less the same as for the watermill. The working force was provided by the wind, which rotated blades connected to a central shaft. Important progress was made when the upper part of the mill was connected to an enormous rotating platform. By turning this in the right way the blades could be perfectly placed to catch every puff of wind, from any direction. Only when there is no wind whatsoever are windmills unable to operate.

Picture of a windmill from a French manuscript of the thirteenth century.

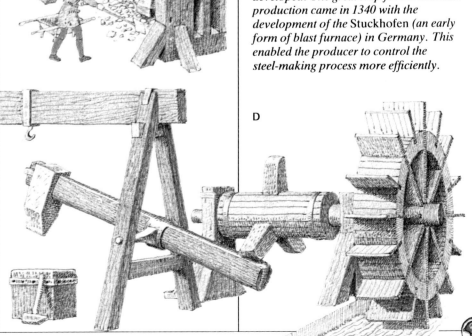

THE BIRTH OF INDUSTRY
Historians say, quite correctly, that the real Industrial Revolution began with the invention of the steam engine and the discovery of electricity, a little more than two centuries ago. But the beginnings of large scale industry appeared in the Middle Ages before that upheaval, as a result of the revival in commerce.

About the year AD 1000 the situation was roughly this: thanks to social and political changes, as well as technological improvements, agriculture produced more than was necessary for survival; that is, a surplus which could be exchanged or sold.

This surplus encouraged some people to buy things that bettered their lives; others to produce and sell goods to grow rich. The introduction of mills made available the energy to work various types of machines which were capable of doing a wide range of tasks automatically. For example, metal-working techniques were revolutionised thanks to the large amounts of energy produced by the mills. A hydraulic wheel and a cam shaft could work huge bellows in a foundry. These blew air into the furnace and raised the temperature high enough to fuse metals which previously had been impossible to melt. Iron, for instance, melts at 1500°C, and in ancient times this temperature could only be reached for a very short time and for a small amount of mineral. In the picture below you can see some of the technological processes of the Middle Ages.

These first industrial workshops produced new materials for the craftsmen to work with.

PROGRESS GENERATES PROGRESS

It is not possible here to mention all the technological innovations of the Middle Ages. Changes in mathematics, cartography and naval techniques improved navigation and were just as important as the mills: we shall discuss these later on. Here we will consider some of the achievements that profoundly changed the lives of the ordinary people.

Spectacles

As a result of the rediscovery of ancient classical works and the spreading of Arab writings on medicine and physiology, various sciences received a new burst of life. One of these was the study of optics.

The invention of spectacles changed the lives of many people. The picture on the right dates from 1352, but the use of concave or convex lenses to improve poor eyesight probably goes back farther than that. It seems that even Emperor Nero, in the first century BC, used some specially shaped precious stones as magnifying lenses.

Xylography

Culture had always been reserved for the privileged few. Despite efforts by the Church and a few enlightened kings only the upper classes learned to read and write. It was generally believed that the peasants and craftsmen didn't need such accomplishments. In any case the lack of manuscripts, and their high cost, limited the spread of formal education.

Two inventions began to change this state of affairs. The first was the technique of carving on wood, or xylography, a process

already known in China. When covered in ink, a design carved on the wood left a clear impression on anything pressed to it. Then, in the fourteenth century, parchment was replaced with a much more useful material – paper! In this way pictures illustrating scenes from the Bible were distributed to people who could not read or write. They were called 'Bibles of the Poor'.

Left: A fresco, dated 1352, showing a cardinal wearing spectacles.
Below: Some alchemists in their laboratory consult obscure Arabic texts to try to find a way of changing common metals into gold.

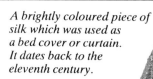

A brightly coloured piece of silk which was used as a bed cover or curtain. It dates back to the eleventh century.

The invention of zero
The science of mathematics also made progress during the Middle Ages. This may have been the field where the greatest steps forward were achieved. Among the many innovations it is worth mentioning the introduction of the Arabic numbers we use today. (Actually, they were really Indian, introduced into Europe by the Arabs.)

The most important number is zero, which though it counts for nothing considerably increased the potential of mathematics.

Using the new numbers merchants were able to keep better accounts.

The birth of chemistry
Medieval alchemists searched for a substance that would change common metals into gold. Today we know that although this is theoretically possible, it is not possible in practice.

However, while searching for this elusive substance the medieval alchemists made thousands and thousands of experiments with a huge range of material and accurately recorded the results. They never found the magic substance, but they discovered the nature of almost all the elements and laid the foundations of the modern science of chemistry.

Gunpowder
The Chinese invented gunpowder. They used it to make fireworks, with which they brightened up the night skies on feast days. It is not known for sure how and when gunpowder was introduced into Europe, but in the fourteenth century it was used on the battlefield. The invention of cannon, using gunpowder to fire stone balls, made quite an impact on enemy forces or against the thick walls of the castles.

Artillery weapons
An unfortunate development of the use of gunpowder was that men realised that the same principles that could be used to design a large cannon and send a cannon ball whizzing through the air could be applied in miniature to produce hand guns. The first hand guns appeared just after the middle of the fourteenth century and were little more than miniature versions of the cannon then in use. They were mounted on wooden handles which were stuck into the ground or rested on the shoulder while the firer applied his match to the touch-hole. However by the first half of the fifteenth century the match-lock appeared. This was a device that led to the development of the trigger which allowed the firer to use both hands to hold and aim his weapon.

The first textile industry
We have left to the end the activity which was the root of the enormous technological and economic development in Europe a few centuries later: the textile industry. The technique of obtaining fibres from sheep's wool and hemp plants (and later from cotton) and weaving them into cloth was a fairly elementary one. So it was the first important human activity to become almost totally industrialised. The rotary and rectilinear movements of the watermill were perfect for the repetitive work of weaving.

The Middle Ages were still a long way away from the huge factories of the nineteenth century. The workshops were small and required only a few workers. But the textile industry produced a great quantity of goods, which were sold by merchants throughout Europe.

'I, Guglielmo Filardo, have in my possession 14 sacks of pepper, weighing 65 cantars and 45 rouleaux; 6 piles of Brazil-wood; 10 pounds of nutmeg; 1 barrel of cinnamon; cloves; spikenard; lacquer. These goods bear the mark of their origin, Alexandria.'

A RICH MERCHANT

Using today's measurements, Guglielmo Filardo, a twelfth-century merchant from Genoa, had the following goods: about 3,300 kilogrammes of pepper (a cantar, a measurement in Turkey and Egypt, was approximately a hundredweight); a quantity of Brazil-wood, much sought-after for its colouring properties; 4.5 kilogrammes of nutmeg; cinnamon; spikenard, an aromatic plant; cloves; and oriental lacquer, used by makers of fine furniture.

In the Middle Ages a merchant specialising in this type of goods would have been a very rich man. As international trade developed the fortunes and power of the bourgeois traders increased.

New trade routes

Filardo's goods came from Alexandria in Egypt. This meant that Europeans – who a century and a half before had feared the end of the world was coming, and who, according to the Arabs, weren't even capable of sailing a plank – were now firmly established on land and sea. The map of trade routes in the Middle Ages shows that commerce had developed all over Europe.

In the North, a strong association of German and Scandinavian towns, the *Hanse*, had a virtual monopoly of the North Sea and the Baltic. In the South, the ports of Genoa, Amalfi and Venice in Italy dominated Mediterranean commerce. These towns benefited from the Crusades, which greatly contributed to the renewal of trade with the East. Caravan trails and sea routes reached even as far as India, south-east Asia and China. The goods from these far-off countries were bought by Europeans in the Islamic ports. In exchange they sold wood, iron, corn, wine, oil and so on.

The *Hanse*, or Hanseatic League, not only controlled trade in the North Sea and the Baltic, they dominated English trade until well into the fifteenth century. In Sweden they had total control of all mining activities and appointed half of the municipal governments.

During the second half of the fifteenth century the League began to decline in

International Trade

A miniature representing a road in the Italian city of Bologna, showing numerous commercial activities including tailors' workshops and shops selling cloth.

power and influence, and as the century advanced political developments in other parts of Europe (particularly in Sweden where Gustav Eriksson rallied the peasants against their Danish overlords) brought about the gradual demise of the League.

Some types of cart used in the Middle Ages: a passenger cart; two carts for transporting goods – one with four wheels, the other with two; a cart with two wheels that could be made longer for carrying more goods.

A four-wheeled passenger carriage

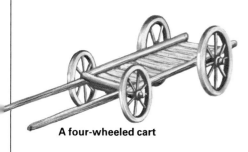

A four-wheeled cart

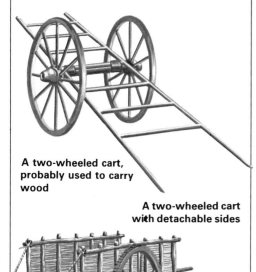

A two-wheeled cart, probably used to carry wood

A two-wheeled cart with detachable sides

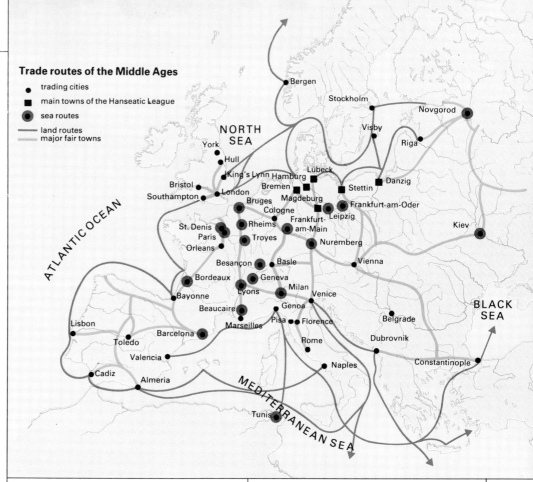

Trade routes of the Middle Ages

- • trading cities
- ■ main towns of the Hanseatic League
- ● sea routes
- —— land routes
- —— major fair towns

NORTH SEA

Bergen
Stockholm
Novgorod
Visby
Riga
York
Hull
King's Lynn   Hamburg   Lübeck   Danzig
Bristol   Bremen   Stettin
Southampton   London   Magdeburg   Frankfurt-am-Oder
Bruges   Cologne
St. Denis   Rheims   Frankfurt-am-Main   Leipzig   Kiev
Paris   Troyes   Nuremberg
Orleans
Besançon   Basle   Vienna
Bordeaux   Geneva
Bayonne   Lyons   Milan   Venice
Beaucaire   Genoa   BLACK SEA
Lisbon   Marseilles   Pisa   Florence   Belgrade
Toledo   Rome   Dubrovnik
Valencia   Naples   Constantinople
Cadiz   Almeria
ATLANTIC OCEAN
MEDITERRANEAN SEA
Barcelona
Tunis

Improvements in transport

Improvements in transport helped the extraordinary boom in European trade which lasted from the eleventh to the fifteenth century.

In land transport, we have already mentioned the shoeing of horses, better harnessing and arranging the horses in line. A band of iron round the wheels of carts and carriages, and an increase in the number of paved roads, were other improvements.

Carts with two wheels, and the heavier four-wheeled carriages, were strong but uncomfortable for travelling in. The floor boarding was directly above the axles of the wheels, which had no springs. So every stone and hole in the road was felt by the unfortunate passenger. By the fourteenth century the bodywork of carriages was suspended by straps, and this absorbed much of the jolting on bad roads. Another problem was that the forecarriage was part of, or fixed to, the body of the cart. This made it difficult to make sharp turns. The invention of a forecarriage that turned round a peg – the first steering system – helped to solve this problem.

A group of merchants would travel together in a company for security: this was called a caravan. The caravans travelled long distances, and as it was inevitable that they would meet outlaws and brigands, the merchants paid an armed escort to travel with them. The travellers themselves often preferred to walk alongside or ride on a horse. Donkeys and mules were usually chosen as pack animals. They were tough and able to withstand difficult conditions, and agile enough to cross mountains and clamber up rough tracks.

It soon became obvious that it was best to use well-worn roads. Some religious orders, notably the Cistercians, dedicated themselves to building and maintaining roads for the good of the people. It was fairly common to see groups of monks laying blocks of stone over layers of sand and gravel. The transportation of goods along rivers, on barges and boats pulled upstream by horses, was much more economical than road transport. Artificial canals were dug to join rivers, using an ingenious system of locks. The feudal lords allowed the boatmen to display their insignia. This was a guarantee of hospitality and protection for the merchants.

Medieval merchants preferred to move their goods by water, either by barge along rivers or in large vessels along the coast of Europe, or even beyond coastal waters. Carriage by water was cheaper than road transport. In England, for example, it was cheaper to import timber from the Baltic than it was to bring it down by road from the Midlands. For the same reason, stone from Normandy was widely used in building castles and cathedrals in southern England. Transport costs were not excessively high compared to the present day. For example, cartage added about 1.5 per cent to the cost of wool in England.

32

At the beginning of the Middle Ages commercial activity was more or less akin to the markets which can still be found in small country towns and villages. From the eleventh and twelfth centuries it began to grow. The first people to be attracted by international commerce were those who, for historic reasons, had always been connected with trade: Jews; Syrians; Byzantines; Levantines, descended from the Phoenicians; and even Arabs. Their success encouraged Europeans to imitate them. Italian, French and Catalan sailors took to the sea in galleys, the size of which followed the so-called 'Catalan rule': tres, dos y as – three, two, one; that is, the length was three times the width, and this was twice the height.

Here we can see a reconstruction of the port of Lübeck, one of the great Hanseatic cities.

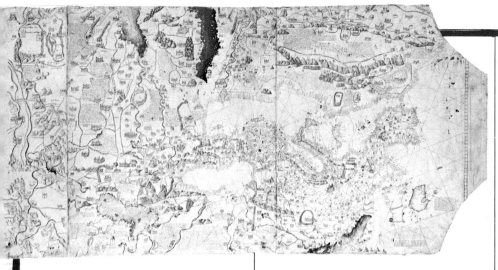

Harbour plans and maritime maps helped to reduce navigational risks. On this map north is at the bottom. To us it seems as if the map is upside-down!

Technological progress in navigation

Medieval trade benefited greatly from improvements in shipbuilding and the introduction of new navigational instruments. The most important innovation was the compass. We are not sure where it originated: the Chinese had known of it for some time, and perhaps it reached Europe via the Arabs. Or it might well have been independently discovered in Europe.

The first to use the compass were the sailors from the commercial city of Amalfi in Italy. Then it spread right through the Mediterranean countries. The magnetised needle, which in early compasses simply floated on water or oil, was later fixed to a pivot which allowed it to rotate freely. With the needle always pointing north, the sailors were able to tackle the open seas without fear of losing their way.

The sailors also began to use two other instruments of Arab origin: the astrolabe and the quadrant, with which they could measure the height of the sun or the stars above the horizon. By carefully calculating their sailing time they could work out how far the ship had moved north or south (latitude) and east or west (longitude). Thanks to these improvements, the Genoese had established a sea route from Italy to Flanders and England by the end of the thirteenth century.

During this period the typical sailing ship of the Mediterranean was the galley. It relied almost exclusively on the wind, though oars were stored in the hull for emergencies. The lateen triangular sail, which could be pointed in any direction, allowed the galley to sail crosswind and even downwind.

The stern-post, a rudder fixed by hinges to the stern of the ship, made manoeuvres a lot easier. A square sail fixed to the triangular one allowed the galley to make full use of starboard winds. The mast could be turned so that it could face lateral winds, and so could the square sail. Some galleys began to use a second mast on the prow.

THE GREAT FAIRS

International trade was concentrated initially in the ports of the North Sea, the Baltic and the Mediterranean. Then gradually it infiltrated the rest of the continent.

Some of the merchants became big business men. They no longer carried a few items of merchandise on the backs of mules, or on carts. They bought complete cargoes wholesale and transported them by boat or pinnace along the rivers and canals. Big business deals were made at the fairs where the merchants gathered. These fairs were the centre of medieval commerce.

The most important were held in London and Stourbridge in England; in Paris, Lyons and Rheims in France; in Ypres, Douai and Bruges in Flanders; Cologne, Frankfurt, Leipzig and Lübeck in Germany; Geneva in Switzerland; and Novgorod in Russia. Each fair lasted six or seven weeks, and they were planned in such a way that when one finished another began in a neighbouring region. In this way the international market was active all the year round.

At the fairs businessmen from Holland, England, Germany and France met others from Italy, Spain and the East. Deals arranged during these meetings stimulated industry and crafts and fostered important innovations in many different fields. The businessmen did not want to carry too much money in their purses, so they exchanged letters of credit: this enabled them to pay debts through an intermediary. So, a business man in Bruges could pay his supplier in Ghent without money having to pass between them. This led to the appearance of cheques, and to the birth of the modern banking and insurance systems. Once again it was the powerful Italian merchant families who came to the forefront. As bankers they were so economically powerful that they could lend enormous sums to kings and popes at a huge interest.

The world was changing rapidly. The feudal castles spread around the countryside lost their importance, while the merchant cities grew. Magnificent buildings surrounded the large squares teeming with people. The fortunes of the once powerful lords declined in favour of the bourgeois merchants, who now held the economic reins in their hands. In a short time the rich and enterprising merchants caused the collapse of the outdated feudal system.

Other changes had occurred which were to have a profound effect on Europe. The invention of printing in Europe was to open up vast opportunities for the spread of knowledge. The use of gunpowder and the invention of cannon held a greater potential for war-making on a much greater scale than had previously been known. Nationalism was beginning to break down the underlying unity of European culture. This unity had been built by the medieval church on the basis that Latin was the language of all learned men.

The life of a knight in England was almost identical to that of a knight in northern France. The life of a peasant in Somerset was almost identical to that of a peasant in a manor in Normandy. The society of Europe of 1400 was almost identical to that of 1000; it was the merchants and the emerging 'middle-class' that were to transform Europe and European society in a way that would have been unthinkable a few centuries before when there was no such group of people as the 'middle class'.

A medieval fair in a small French town. Fairs were different from markets because they lasted longer, often for several weeks; and because trade was done wholesale. The fairs were held in places specially designed to receive the merchants and their goods. Because of the large amounts of money that changed hands they were centres of prosperity. For this reason they were encouraged by kings and lords, who granted the participants special privileges, such as exemption from taxes.

'What strange times we live in! The world is turning upside-down! The people have dispossessed the clergy and the nobles of their right to collect taxes. In exchange for a certain sum they are forced to concede the right to set up a commune.

Commune: a detestable word! Everyone who, a short time ago, was subject to feudal obligations is now free of the allegiance he owes to his lord and pays a duty only once a year. Anyone who breaks the law gets away with a small penalty. . . .'

These are the words of an abbot, Gilbert Nogent, who lived in France during the twelfth century.

The revolt of the bourgeoisie

In previous chapters we spoke of the economic revival in Western Europe; the growth of the ancient *burgs* into real cities; and the increasing importance of their inhabitants, the burghers, or bourgeoisie. In the main European cities trade associations were formed, called guilds, companies or corporations. At the beginning their aim was to protect members of the same trade from the dangers of external competition; to help those in need; and to guarantee the standard of their work. But the members soon realised that their most dangerous enemies were the feudal lords. The struggle between the emerging bourgeoisie and the lords was at the root of the development of free European communes.

The bourgeoisie were no longer content to accept the dictates of the aristocracy without comment – they wanted a say in how they were governed.

ASSEMBLIES OR PARLIAMENTS
Rich and influential citizens first began governing themselves in places where the feudal lord's control was less harsh, as in the Italian coastal cities. They set up an assembly, or parliament, to establish a statute and rules for governing the city. They then elected representatives who, for a certain number of months or years ruled the community. All the people swore to respect the authority of their representatives and to defend the independence of the commune. This is the way in which most of the free communes were set up. They were called 'sworn' communes because the members were bound by an oath of loyalty. Communes were unknown in England, where the monarch exercised absolute authority until well into the seventeenth century.

The Age of the Commune

COMMUNE: A NEW, DETESTABLE WORD . . .

Why was the abbot so outraged? Why were the communes so detestable? In his eyes it was appalling that the ordinary people, who until then had been subject to the feudal lord's authority, should begin to govern themselves in communes.

Gilbert Nogent was not alone in his condemnation: most of the feudal lords themselves, the bishops and even the pope himself thought the same way.

But the disapproval of the clergy and the nobles did not stop the communes spreading throughout France, in Flanders, Germany, Northern Italy, Spain, and all over Europe. It was a decisive step forward to the formation of a more modern social and political system.

What were the reasons for the spread of this powerful movement?

Trade guilds were particularly well organised in the free communes.
Above left: the emblem of the moneychangers of Perugia in Italy.
The communes had their own money and organised their own troops.
Above right: a coin from the commune of Brescia.
Below: a bas-relief showing Milanese citizens in arms.

THE CITY AIR LIBERATES . . .

'The noble city of Bologna, which has always fought for freedom . . . remembering the past and looking forward to the future . . . has freed for a cash payment everyone who lived in conditions of slavery in the city and diocese of Bologna. They have been declared free citizens; and from now on no servant or slave will live on Bolognese territory, neither will anyone try to hold in bondage men who are free by nature . . .'

This document from the city of Bologna was dated 1257, but it had taken several decades to arrive at such a civilised decision.

It was said that 'the city air liberates them'. In fact, a rule which was accepted everywhere stated that if a serf escaped from his feudal lord and managed to take refuge in a free commune for a year and a day he automatically became free.

Progressive emancipation

Communes grew up where prosperous city bourgeoisie managed to control, or effectively neutralise, the power of the feudal lords. However it was not the only way of achieving this goal.

Sometimes the citizens found a powerful ally in the bishop who lived in the city. Whether it was because of his religious convictims to help the poor, defenceless people, or for political reasons, the bishop took the citizens' side and did not hesitate to take up arms and fight the overbearing feudal lords.

This happened in Milan, which became one of the first and most powerful communes in Europe. Around the year 1000 the Milanese had already rallied to their bishop, Ariberto di Intimiano, who in a short time freed them from their feudal lords. This was not all: when Emperor Con-rad II moved into Italy in 1037 to bring them back into line, Ariberto managed to beat him, with the help of the people. In this battle the famous *Carroccio*, the altar-wagon over which flew the flags of the city militia, was used. It later became the symbol of the commune.

Eight years later the Milanese got rid of the bishop and freely elected representatives governed the commune.

Freedom papers

In other places the people took action of their own accord. Every spring the communal army – composed of all citizens able to carry arms and led by elected officers – made sorties into the surrounding countryside. The military objective was to destroy the castles of the feudal lords. The political objective was to induce the lord to move

into the city, where it would be easier to control him.

The feudal lords often accepted money in exchange for giving up their rights. These dispossessed nobles gave the communes freedom papers, or charters, which listed the rights of free communes.

Kings and emperors gave similar charters to certain rich cities, thus binding the city to them and destroying the power of the feudal lords.

Organisation of the commune

Having achieved autonomy, the communes were organised under the government of magistrates, helped by a council largely made up of the richest and most influential citizens.

Sometimes harsh conflicts broke out between the trade corporations and the 'big men' of the city: bankers, merchants, or old feudal lords who were still rich and wanted to command the people.

These struggles sometimes became so violent that the king or emperor would step in and take control. Or – as happened in Italy in the middle of the twelfth century – a foreigner who could be objective was entrusted with the governing of the commune. This foreigner was given the title *podestà*, meaning one who exercises authority.

This system worked for several decades but it went against the principles of the free commune. To keep the peace and pander to the interests of a few, the liberty of everyone was sacrificed by handing power to a single 'strong man'. Everything was fine as long as he was objective, just and incorruptible; but if he wasn't. . .

While it lasted, the movement of emanci-pation of the common people had a great influence on medieval society. It introduced ways of thinking and attitudes which were completely different from feudal times, and left a legacy which has survived right up to the present day: local government.

In some countries, like Germany, the free towns banded together in leagues, or Hanses. In Alsace ten communes formed the Decapole.

The drawing below shows one of these cities, with its characteristic architecture. The walls of the buildings were covered with wooden structures like trellises.

A RICH CITY-COMMUNE
The free communes spread and prospered throughout Europe thanks to trade, crafts, industry, agriculture, and entrepreneurial skills.

Let's take a modern family as an example. When, by working hard, the family manages to acquire a good standard of living, what happens? It wants to buy luxury goods that are not essentials of life: perhaps new furniture for the house to make it more comfortable. It thinks of 'needs' that didn't exist before: to listen to music, look at paintings, take a holiday . . .

Something similar happened, on a larger scale, in the rich communal cities. Not only work but art, learning, technology – a new civilisation prospered. These changes were reflected in the appearance of the cities. This fourteenth-century fresco by Ambrogio Lorenzetti shows the Italian city of Siena.

The city was surrounded by strong walls, financed by the bourgeoisie. Inside the walls the roads were straight and narrow. The houses were built back-to-back; here and there were towers belonging to the richest families.

The typical house had a large living-room on the ground floor opening on to a small courtyard, and bedrooms on the upper floor.

In the centre of the city stood the cathedral. All the citizens contributed to its building, either materially or financially. The market square near the cathedral was the principal meeting place. And not far away was the communal palace, also built with everybody's help. In some parts of Europe, like Flanders or Artois, it was called the belfry, and was the symbol of the free commune.

The public fountain provided a free supply of water. In parts of the city away from the fountain, water was sold in earthenware pots.

The craft workshops opened directly on to the roads. In good weather the craftsmen displayed their work and often worked outside.

On market days peasants brought their produce to sell in the city. The commune's officials controlled the price and the quality. In this way the power of the commune extended into the countryside, replacing the power of the feudal lord.

December

During the Middle Ages the peasants had a concept of time that was rather different from our own. They thought it was something that continually repeated itself, always returning to where it started, like the hands of a clock. The idea of progress, of constant movement towards something better, was totally alien to them.

Time was cyclical, like the seasons, repeating itself over and over again. The peasants' calendar took the form of a succession of agricultural activities: ploughing, sowing and harvesting provided the rhythm of their lives.

This agricultural calendar was also adhered to by the townspeople.

THE UNKNOWN PEOPLE WHO MADE HISTORY

Emperors, kings, popes, famous warriors and rich merchants – the important people of medieval history accounted for only five per cent of society. Who were the other ninety-five per cent of the population? Most of them were the peasants who worked on the land.

From ancient times, and right up to the beginning of the nineteenth century, peasants were the roots of society, the basis of economic activity and of European civilisation. The ambitious merchants and craftsmen were responsible for the prosperity of medieval cities, but it was the peasants who provided their essential food.

Agricultural work was laborious, restricting, and monotonous; but as it became more and more efficient it helped Europe to survive and prosper. The people who lived on the land are rarely mentioned by historians, but they were the unknown makers of medieval history.

Peasants in the Middle Ages

A motif of the months of the year was often used on sculptures, stained glass windows and miniatures during the Middle Ages. The appropriate agricultural activities symbolised the different months. Here is a series of French miniatures from the thirteenth century, showing, from left to right above and below, December, September, July, August and June.

In December the pig was killed and roasted. September was the month of the grape harvest. The grapes were put into large barrels and crushed by foot to make wine. In July weeding was carried out with special tools. August was the time for reaping and gathering in the grain. June was hay-making time: the peasants cut it with scythes and piled it into heaps with forks.

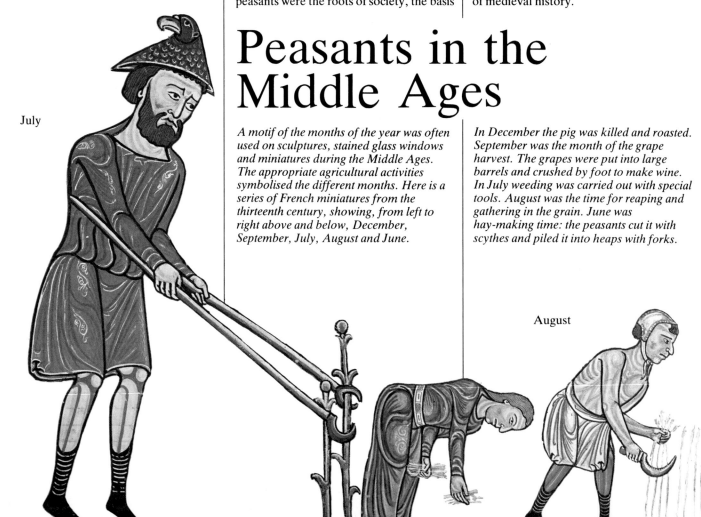

July

August

September

41

The serfs of the glebe

The peasants, or serfs of the glebe – that is, of the soil – were part of a manor or farm. When it was sold they passed to the new owner, along with the animals belonging to the farm. The son of a peasant had but one path open to him: to become a peasant like his parents and grandparents, just as his sons and grandsons would become in their turn.

The serfs were not actually slaves, but they lived in conditions that were very close to those of the ancient slaves.

Since the fall of the Roman Empire slavery had declined under the influence of the new social order. The Church, too, condemned slavery.

The serfs had many duties, but they also had rights: they were considered to be people, and not just things. (The Greek philosopher, Aristotle, had described slaves as 'living, working instruments'.) There was no law that tied them to the land: in theory they could leave the manor of the feudal lord whenever they pleased.

An historian of the Middle Ages wrote: 'Serfs enjoy this privilege: they cannot be thrown off the land.' Was it therefore a privilege to be a serf? Perhaps it was!

Words as documents

Serfs were universal all over Northern Europe. Evidence of this is found in the vocabulary of many European languages. From the Latin word *maneo*, meaning 'I remain', comes manor or manse – the farm and fields where the peasant lived and worked.

In France the peasants were called *manants* – those who 'remained' on the land. The word for house is *maison*.

In Italy the word *mansione* meant the tasks the serf had to carry out.

We do not know a great deal about the conditions of serfs in some countries. In Spain, for example, little is known of the details of manorial cultivation. We know that slaves played an important part in the working of the land, and in the early fifteenth century there was a well-known and busy market for human slaves in Catalonia.

In eastern Europe settlements were extremely small, often only four or six households. The records of the monastery of Vladimir show that they had tenants who performed such services as threshing and net-making and that slave labour was important.

Country and town: the gap widens

During the Middle Ages the difference between town and country was not as great as it is today. Around the city walls, and even inside them, were fields, meadows and vegetable gardens. Almost everybody worked a piece of land or kept animals.

But technical specialisation, accentuated by economic activities – commerce, industry, administrative and intellectual work in the city, cultivation and animal husbandry in the country – opened up a gulf which gradually widened. The different types of activity produced different ways of thinking.

The life of the peasants was governed by the seasons, the same jobs being repeated from one year to the next. Time was cyclical – always returning to the point of departure, according to the season. Changes in the countryside were fewer than in the towns.

City life, on the other hand, meant more social contact: the spread of intellectual ideas and new techniques of work. People who lived in the city seemed to be freer, less restricted by the forces of nature than the peasants were.

They were also free to choose what they wanted to do – no lords of the manor held power over them.

June

MAN-MADE EUROPE

At the beginning of the Middle Ages Europe was a vast expanse of wild and uncultivated land, ravaged by the incursions of barbarian invaders.

The transformation of the continent was the result of years of uninterrupted work begun during the Middle Ages, particularly the massive clearing of forest land that took place from the eleventh century in Burgundy, North Germany and the area around Paris. The face of Europe today was made by man.

The basic unit: the manse

The land belonging to the feudal lord was divided into two parts. The first was the lord's domain, from the Latin *dominus*, meaning master. As well as the castle or manor house it consisted of fields, vineyards, pastureland, forests and hunting ground. The village around the castle, with the bakehouse, the mill, and the workshops of those who served the community – the blacksmith, carpenter, saddler, and so on – also belonged to the lord's domain.

The rest of the land was split into farms, or manses, held in tenure by one or several families. The manse was the basic unit of the agricultural economy of the Middle Ages. The home and kitchen garden of the peasant were also included.

The produce from the kitchen garden be-longed to the serf, as did the meat from his pig. This was his and his family's main source of animal protein, since oxen were used for work and sheep were kept for their wool.

The serf had the right to graze his animals on fallow ground, uncultivated land and the lord's forest. He could also gather wood for his fire.

The serf's duties

In return for the land and military protection the serf had to give the lord part of his harvest, to pay taxes, and to perform certain duties, called corvées, free of charge. These might be ploughing, hoeing, harvesting, or cutting the hay. Other work was done by paid agricultural labourers.

The serfs also had to take the lord's produce to market; to act as couriers or messengers when required; and to do special jobs such as building bridges and roads, digging wells or repairing the castle walls.

From serfdom to rent

The feudal lords' need for money increased as a result of the general prosperity which made available a greater range of goods in the markets. They also needed money to pay the wages of the agricultural labourers and the soldiers.

We already know that the peasants made a bit of money by selling the products they

didn't need, at the market. This profit helped to change their relationship with the feudal lord. By paying him a certain sum they could free themselves, at least in part, of the corvées, and of military obligations.

Later on, over a long period, lords and peasants all over Europe began to prefer a relationship based on rent rather than on serfdom. This meant that the peasant paid money to the lord as rent, in exchange for the land.

The amount of money paid, the dates of payments and all the other conditions of the contract were written down in a book – the *libellus* or *livellus* was its Latin name at that time.

The number of peasants who bought their freedom increased as the Middle Ages advanced, and as a result production increased. The farmers were much more in-

On the left: a medieval peasant with a wooden fork and a sickle.
Below, left: open field system of Northern Europe. Below, right: fields enclosed by walls in Italy.
These two types of medieval agriculture are still used today. On the damp, heavy soils of Northern Europe ploughing long furrows in large open fields helps to aerate the soil and evaporate excess moisture. In the drier areas of the Mediterranean the walls help to keep in the moisture.

terested in improving production when everything except the rent belonged to them.

The 'third field'

Since ancient times the peasants had known that certain crops, especially cereals, sapped the land while others – legumes such as beans and peas, the medieval peasants' basic food – enriched it.

To stop the soil becoming impoverished ancient farmers used the biennial crop rotation system: one year a cereal was grown in a field and the following year it was left fallow – ploughed but not sown – so that the soil could become fertile again. Peasants of the Middle Ages introduced the system of the 'third field', in effect a triennial rotation. A field was sown with cereals the first year (winter sowing), then with vegetables the next year (spring sowing), and the third year it was left to rest. Whilst with the old system one field out of two was unproductive, now it was one field out of three.

Bearing in mind the fact that the second field of spring-sown vegetables enriched the soil with nutrients as well as providing basic foodstuffs, the increase in productivity must have been around fifty per cent.

This meant an increase in food supplies and more to sell in the market. The existence of the peasant farmers became less precarious because it was unlikely that bad

weather would destroy two crops in the same year and the chances were that both crops, spring and autumn, would be harvested. All in all the lifestyle of the peasants was considerably improved.

The increased yield of the earth and of labour removed the economic necessity for dividing villages into demesnes and tenures. Commercialisation spread from the town to the country. Farmers began to specialise, choosing crops that were best suited to their soil. Regions such as Sicily and parts of Germany provided corn for other areas where there were shortages. Gascony produced wine not just for the people who lived there, but to export to non-wine-producing areas. Huge parts of England and Castile were given over to rearing sheep to supply wool. Some valleys in Italy concentrated solely on cultivating plants for medicines and dyes. Market gardens and orchards sprang up around the towns.

The Middle Ages had begun with the exploitation of slaves and the toil of poor farmers to benefit a small élite. The late Middle Ages reduced the toil through improved techniques and spread the profits a little more evenly among the classes. It did not solve the problem of poverty among the poorer peasants, but it did enable other members of society to improve their standards of living and devote more time to leisure and pleasure.

CULTURE DURING THE DARK AGES

The tales told by the minstrels were not the only source of culture for the ordinary people. There was a great oral tradition of handing down, from father to son and mother to daughter, tales, legends, proverbs, herbal remedies . . . and to all this was added the teachings of the Church.

This popular culture was a mixture of truth and fantasy, and the dividing line between them was thin. Tales were told of fabulous animals, superhuman deeds, fantastic countries. . .

The author of a famous book, *Liber Monstrorum* (Book of Marvels), for example, knew that most of the stories the people heard were incredible, and he wrote: 'You could only prove they were false if you had a pair of wings and went to find out. Take the case of the golden city, or the beach covered in jewels we hear so much about: you would only find a city of stone (if the city exists at all) and a beach of pebbles.'

Then the author added: 'I write only about things that are in some way credible.' The concept of credibility and truth was already important to the educated men.

Reading and writing: privileges of a few

At that time there were no newspapers, magazines, radio or television. There were books, but no printing presses. The books were written by hand by monk-scribes, who took a year or more to write or copy a single work.

They wrote on sheets of parchment made from specially treated lambs' skin (the best ones) or from sheep's skin.

The books were so expensive that they were luxury items. In the twelfth century Bernard de Chartres, a renowned scholar,

Science and Culture

Some studious pupils listen attentively to the words of their master: they are in a cathedral school of the Middle Ages, gathered in the cloisters. The students are sitting on bales of straw with wax tablets on their knees: the master stands in front. Later, in the fourteenth century, they would sit on benches and use parchment to write on. The youngest pupils are nine or ten years old; the oldest thirteen or fourteen. Sometimes a few adults join them for lessons. Those students were only a minority. In the Middle Ages culture was spread by word of mouth, by the church and by the wandering minstrels who visited the castles. For the favoured few, universities opened in the eleventh and twelfth centuries: at Bologna in Italy, Oxford and Cambridge in England, Heidelberg in Germany, and the Sorbonne in Paris, all still thriving today.

had a wonderful library . . . of twenty-four volumes! The Italian Francesco Accursio, a well-known student of law, owned the incredible number of sixty-three. These learned men really did possess a treasure, because a Bible in those days was sold for the equivalent of about £8,000; a missal was exchanged for a vineyard; and two volumes of ancient Roman grammar were valued at the price of a house and a field.

There were very few books, but then few people could read and even less could write. Throughout the Middle Ages illiteracy was the fate of the majority of the population all over Europe.

At that time illiteracy did not bother anyone: reading and writing were specialised trades. If anyone needed to read a letter or know the contents of a legal document, or to write anything, he went to a specialist. In the same way that today we are not surprised if a prime minister does not know how to weave and sew, no one then was surprised if kings and princes were illiterate, let alone the craftsmen and peasants.

The Church and culture

Amongst all this ignorance, the Church stood out as the only cultural institution of the time, a meeting place between ancient classical knowledge and modern culture.

Left: a bas-relief showing students having a lesson.
Below: a minstrel amusing the crowds at a tournament. Minstrels sang of the marvellous adventures of the Knights of the Round Table and other medieval heroes.

An historian of the time wrote: 'Bishops and monks sit in assemblies alongside generals and kings. They are the only ones who know how to make a speech and hold a pen in their hands. Secretaries, counsellors and theologians participate in drawing up edicts. . . . In churches and monasteries they preserve the conquests of the human race: the Latin language, literature, sculpture, art, and – most precious of all – the techniques that guarantee man his bread, his clothes, and his house . . .'

As early as the sixth century, during the time of the barbarian invasions, St Benedict counselled his monks to learn how to read and write, to keep a library in the monastery and add to it by copying out ancient manuscripts, and to open an elementary school for anyone to attend whenever it was possible. Thanks to people like him this philosophy – multiplied in dozens of churches and monasteries in the following centuries – helped to spread culture.

The ecclesiastical schools

Charlemagne ordered that priests should open free schools in every parish. While the monk scribes in dozens of monasteries saved ancient manuscripts by copying them on to parchment, schools multiplied near cathedrals, churches and the monasteries.

The essential role of these schools was to produce future clerics.

The bishops, at the time of the third Lateran Council in 1179, had ordered that: 'so as not to deprive poor children of the chance to read and better themselves . . . in every cathedral a certain sum should be set aside to pay a master to teach the clerics and poor students for nothing.'

In fact there were almost always two schools near each cathedral. The first was for those who wished to study and join the Church, the second was an elementary school. The latter was very important as it was free and open to anyone: children of the rich and of peasants, aspiring monks who were still too young for the monasteries, craftsmen and merchants.

Such schools played an important role in spreading learning throughout Europe.

The schools of these days were quite unlike the schools of today. There were very few, if any, books available for the students to read and study from. In England there was little formal education for the ordinary people.

The only chance that a boy had of going to school was if he was clever enough to study for holy orders. In this case the local priest would teach him the basics of Latin before he went off to study.

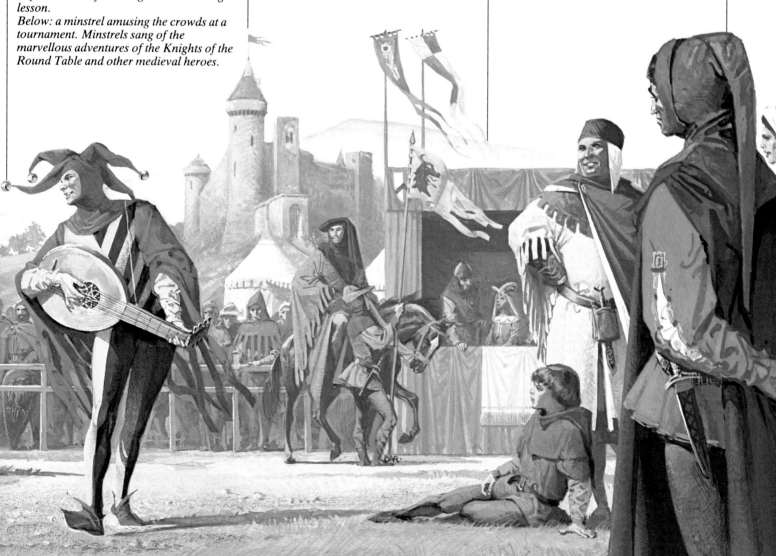

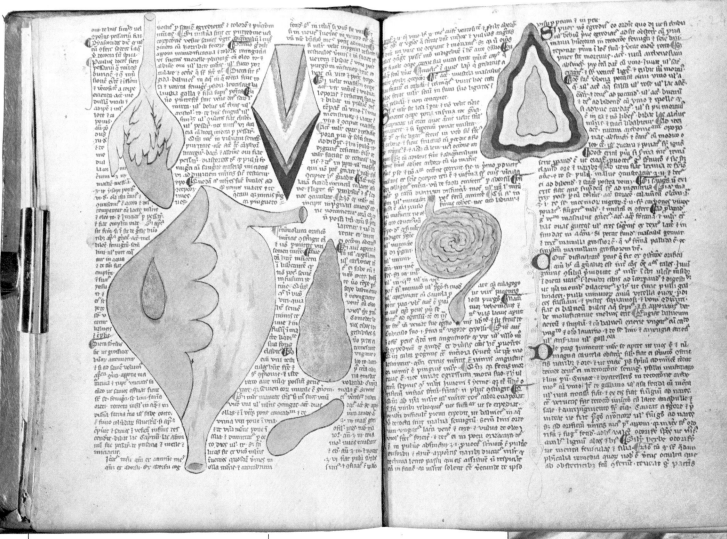

THE FIRST UNIVERSITIES

Having received a grounding in grammar, arithmetic, geometry, music and theology in an elementary school, the student could continue his studies at a university. Medieval universities were rather different from modern ones. A group of students of various nationalities would get together and pay a master themselves. The doctors, or professors, often lodged the students under their own roof. But as they were paid directly by the students, their earnings depended on the reputation they gained.

Being a professor in the Middle Ages wasn't always easy: if he explained himself badly, or was boring, or made a mistake, he was booed and sometimes even beaten up.

Ignorant people wanting to learn

Medieval people were ignorant and gullible, superstitious and devout. They believed in magic, witches and good luck charms as well as in God.

The common people, as well as the clerics and university students, were hungry for knowledge. A dispute between two professors over religion, philosophy or science rapidly became a collective discussion. From the university it soon reached the taverns, where the dispute often turned into a heated discussion, or even a brawl. The clergy and students were a separate social category linked by their love of knowledge. They spoke together in Latin, the international language, and travelled in groups all over Europe. Although they were not always well received, these groups of exuberant wandering students played an important role in spreading knowledge and shaping an international culture.

Above and to the right: pages from a medieval medical book. They show sketches of the heart, the liver, the intestines and the human skeleton. Medicine became a subject of study and was taught in the universities. The first books on hygiene and herbal remedies appeared, and people began to understand more about human anatomy. Despite these advances the people still believed in the existence of strange creatures like the ones shown alongside.

What did they study in the Middle Ages?

The professors were interested, first and foremost, in theology, that is the study of God and His work, of man and his destiny. Thomas Aquinas at the Sorbonne had a profound influence on theology during the thirteenth century. After that, philosophy, the study of ideas. Philosophy became popular thanks to the Arabs, who had saved the works of the great Greek philosophers, particularly Aristotle, and translated them. Oxford University established a reputation as a centre for philosophical studies. Alongside these two disciplines other practical sciences developed, connected with everyday needs. Contact with the Arab world, and in particular the school of medicine at Baghdad, resulted in some of the great European schools of medicine. Salerno in Italy, Seville in Spain and Montpellier in France all became centres of medicine.

Around 1240 all those who wanted to study medicine in the kingdom of Sicily had to follow the course laid down by the king, Frederick II. Three years of logic, five years of medicine, including surgery and anatomy, and one year's probation with a qualified doctor – nine years in all, before the student was allowed to practise independently. Certificates had been issued to doctors since Norman times, but Frederick was the first to decree that royal officials had no right to issue a certificate to a doctor except with the approval of the professors at Salerno.

The school at Salerno became the most important medical school in Europe until it was eclipsed in the thirteenth century by the newer schools at Montpellier, Padua and, above all, at Bologna. Whereas at Salerno, the students learned anatomy from books and dissected animals, at Bologna the medical students had to witness the dissection of a human corpse at least once a year. Medicine was, at this time, quite primitive. The doctors knew a great deal about anatomy, but knew nothing of the circulation of the blood. Physiology was dominated by the belief that the body was composed of the four humours – melancholic, sanguinic, phlegmatic and choleric.

Pathology was successful in describing and distinguishing symptoms of illnesses, but not so good at identifying their causes and remedies. Pharmacology was skilful in the preparation of herbal remedies, but clumsy in the use of chemical compounds.

There were, however, excellent surgeons who performed some remarkable operations and one professor at Bologna, Hugh Borgognoni, introduced a radical treatment of wounds. Instead of making them suppurate by applying greasy ointments, he suggested that they should be cleaned and disinfected with wine.

A remarkable discovery was made around the middle of the fourteenth century. During an epidemic of the plague, which killed a third of the population, some Italian doctors discovered that the disease spread rapidly when healthy people came in contact with sick ones. The first step had been taken towards controlling infectious illnesses. At the same time the development of commerce, and the need to keep accounts, encouraged the study of mathematics. Enormous progress was made.

Thus the medieval sages prepared the ground for the enormous leap forward in culture, science and technology that took place from the fifteenth century.

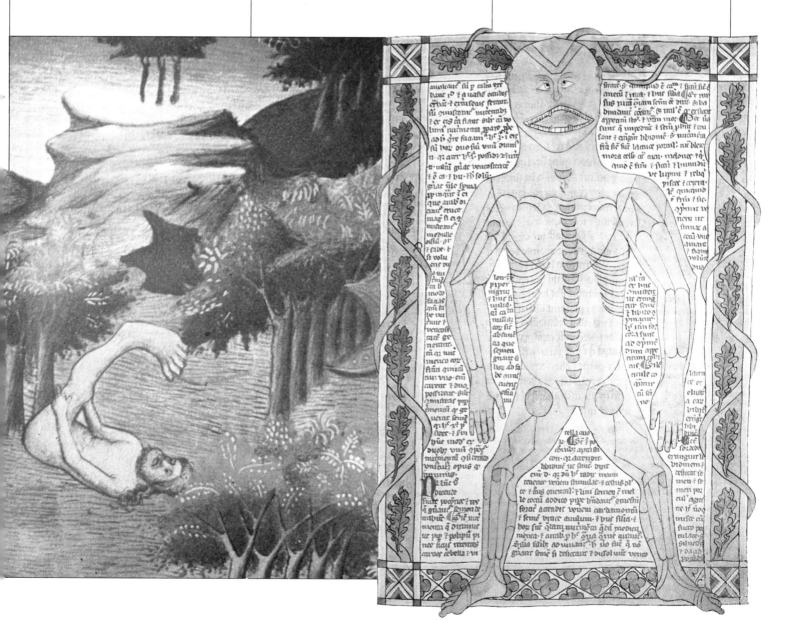